MISTER ROBERTS

BY THOMAS HEGGEN
AND JOSHUA LOGAN

★

★

DRAMATISTS
PLAY SERVICE
INC.

MISTER ROBERTS was first presented by Leland Hayward at the Alvin Theatre, New York City, on February 18, 1948, with the following cast:

(IN ORDER OF APPEARANCE)

CHIEF JOHNSON	Rusty Lane
LIEUTENANT (JG) ROBERTS	Henry Fonda
DOC	Robert Keith
DOWDY	Joe Marr
THE CAPTAIN	William Harrigan
INSIGNA	Harvey Lembeck
MANNION	Ralph Meeker
LINDSTROM	Karl Lukas
STEFANOWSKI	Steven Hill
WILEY	Robert Baines
SCHLEMMER	Lee Krieger
REBER	John Campbell
ENSIGN PULVER	David Wayne
DOLAN	Casey Walters
GERHART	Fred Barton
PAYNE	James Sherwood
LIEUTENANT ANN GIRARD	Jocelyn Brando
SHORE PATROLMAN	John Jordan
MILITARY POLICEMAN	Marshall Jamison
SHORE PATROL OFFICER	Murray Hamilton

SEAMEN, FIREMEN and OTHERS: Tiger Andrews, Joe Bernard, Ellis Eringer, Mikel Kane, Bob Keith, Jr., Walter Mullen, John (Red) Kullers, Jack Pierce, Len Smith, Jr., Sanders (Sandy) Turner

DIRECTED BY Joshua Logan

SETTINGS AND LIGHTING BY Jo Mielziner

NOTE: The roles of Reber, Payne and Schlemmer may be broken up and split as the director sees fit, and shared among two actors, if desired.

SCENE

Aboard the U. S. Navy Cargo Ship, *AK 601*, operating in the back areas of the Pacific.

TIME: A few weeks before V-E Day until a few weeks before V-J Day.

NOTE: In the U. S. Navy, all officers below the rank of Commander are addressed as " Mister."

MISTER ROBERTS

ACT I

SCENE 1

The curtain rises on the main set, which is the amidships section of a navy cargo ship. The section of the ship shown is the house, and the deck immediately forward of the house. Dominating C. *stage is a covered hatch. The house extends on an angle to the audience from downstage* L. *to upstage* R. *At each side is a passageway leading to the after part of the ship. Over the passageways on each side are twenty-millimeter gun tubs, ladders lead up to each tub. In each passageway and hardly visible to the audience is a steep ladder leading up to a bridge. Downstage* R. *is a double bitt. At the* L. *end of the hatch cover is an opening. This is the entrance to the companionway which leads to the crew's compartment below. The lower parts of two kingposts are shown against the house. A life raft is also visible. A solid metal rail runs from stage* R. *and disappears behind the house. Upstage* C. *is the door to the* CAPTAIN'S *cabin. The pilothouse with its many portholes is indicated on the bridge above. On the flying bridge are the usual nautical furnishings: a searchlight and two ventilators. Over the door is a loudspeaker. There is a porthole to the* L. *of the door and two portholes to the* R. *These last two look into the* CAPTAIN'S *cabin. The only object which differentiates this ship from any other navy cargo ship is a small scrawny palm tree, potted in a five-gallon can, standing to the right of the* CAPTAIN'S *cabin door. On the container, painted in large white letters, is the legend: " PROP.T OF CAPTAIN, KEEP AWAY."*

At rise, the lighting indicates that it is shortly after dawn. The stage is empty and there is no indication of life other than the sound of snoring from below. CHIEF

5

JOHNSON, *a bulging man about forty, enters through passageway upstage* L. *He wears dungaree shirt and pants and a chief petty officer's cap. He is obviously chewing tobacco, and he starts down the hatchway, notices the palm tree, crosses to the* CAPTAIN'S *door cautiously, peering into the porthole to see that he is not being watched, then deliberately spits into the palm tree container. He wipes his mouth smugly and shuffles over to the hatch. There he stops, takes out his watch and looks at it, then disappears down the hatchway. A shrill whistle is heard.*

JOHNSON. (*Offstage—in a loud singsong voice which is obviously just carrying out a ritual.*) Reveille . . . Hit the deck . . . Greet the new day . . . (*The whistle is heard again.*) Reveille . . .

INSIGNA. (*Offstage.*) Okay, Chief, you done your duty—now get your big fat can out of here! (JOHNSON *reappears at the head of hatchway calling back.*)

JOHNSON. Just thought you'd like to know about reveille. And you're going to miss chow again. (*His duty done,* JOHNSON, *still chewing, shuffles across the stage and disappears. There is a brief moment of silence, then the snoring is resumed below. After a moment,* ROBERTS *enters from the passageway at* R. *He wears khaki shirt and trousers and an officer's cap. On each side of his collar he wears the silver bar indicating the rank of Lieutenant [junior grade]. He carries a rumpled piece of writing paper in his left hand, on which there is a great deal of writing and large black marks indicating that much has been scratched out. He walks slowly to the bitt, concentrating, then stands a moment looking out* R. *He suddenly gets an idea and goes to hatch cover, sitting and writing on the paper.* DOC *enters from the* L. *passageway.* DOC *is between thirty-five and forty and he wears khakis and an officer's fore-and-aft cap, he wears medical insignia and the bars of Lieutenant [senior grade] on his collar. A stethoscope sticks out of his hip pocket. He is wiping the sweat off his neck with his handkerchief as he crosses above hatch cover. He stops as he sees* ROBERTS.)

DOC. That you, Doug?

ROBERTS. (*Wearily, looking up.*) Hello, Doc. What are you doing up?

6

DOC. I heard you were working cargo today so I thought I'd get ready. On days when there's any work to be done I can always count on a big turnout at sick call.

ROBERTS. (*Smiles.*) Oh, yeah.

DOC. I attract some very rare diseases on cargo days. That day they knew you were going to load five ships I was greeted by six more cases of beriberi—double beriberi—whatever that is. (*He sits on hatch cover.*)

ROBERTS. What are you giving them these days for double beriberi?

DOC. Aspirin—what else? (*He looks at* ROBERTS.) Is there something wrong, Doug?

ROBERTS. (*Preoccupied.*) No.

DOC. (*Lying back on the hatch.*) We missed you when you went on watch last night. I gave young Ensign Pulver another drink of alcohol and orange juice and it inspired him to relate further sexual feats of his. Some of them bordered on the supernatural!

ROBERTS. I don't doubt it. Did he tell you how he conquered a forty-five-year-old virgin by the simple tactic of being the first man in her life to ask her a direct question?

DOC. No. Last night he was more concerned with quantity. It seems that on a certain cold and wintry night—a night when most of us mortal men would have settled for a cup of cocoa—he made life worth living for three girls in Washington, D. C., caught the 11:45 train, and an hour later performed the same humanitarian service for a young lady in Baltimore.

ROBERTS. (*Laughing.*) Good Lord!

DOC. I'm not sure what to do with young Pulver. I'm thinking of reporting his record to the American Medical Association. Say, there *is* something wrong, isn't there?

ROBERTS. I've been up all night, Doc.

DOC. What is it? What's the matter?

ROBERTS. I saw something last night when I was on watch that just about knocked me out.

DOC. (*Alarmed.*) What happened?

ROBERTS. (*With emotion.*) I was up on the bridge. I was just standing there looking out to sea. I couldn't bear to look at that island any more. All of a sudden I noticed something. Little black specks crawling over the horizon. I looked through the glasses

7

and it was a formation of our ships that stretched for miles! Carriers and battleships and cans—a whole task force, Doc!

DOC. Why didn't you break me out? I've never seen a battleship!

ROBERTS. They came on and they passed within half a mile of that reef! Carriers so big they blacked out half the sky! And battle-wagons sliding along—dead quiet! I could see the men on the bridges. And this is what knocked me out, Doc. Somehow—I thought I was on those bridges—I thought I was riding west across the Pacific. I watched them until they were out of sight, Doc—and I was right there on those bridges all the time.

DOC. I know how that must have hurt, Doug.

ROBERTS. And then I looked down from our bridge and saw our Captain's palm tree! (*Points at palm tree, then bitterly.*) Our trophy for superior achievement! The Admiral John J. Finchley award for delivering more toothpaste and toilet paper than any other Navy cargo ship in the safe area of the Pacific. (*Taking letter from pocket and handing it to* DOC.) Read this, Doc—see how it sounds.

DOC. What is it?

ROBERTS. My application for transfer. I've been rewriting it all night.

DOC. Good Lord, not another one!

ROBERTS. This one's different. It's got stronger wording. Read it. (DOC *looks for a moment skeptically, then noticing the intensity in his face decides to read the letter.*)

DOC. (*Reading.*) "From: Lieutenant (jg) Douglas Roberts. To: Bureau of Naval Personnel. Subject: Change of Duty, Request for . . ." (*He looks up.*) Boy, this is sheer poetry.

ROBERTS. (*Rises nervously.*) Go on, Doc.

DOC. (*Reads on.*) "For two years and four months I have served aboard this vessel as Cargo Officer. I feel that my continued service aboard can only increase disharmony aboard this ship." (*He looks at* ROBERTS *and rises.* ROBERTS *looks back defiantly.*)

ROBERTS. How about that!

DOC. (*Whistles softly, then continues.*) "I therefore urgently request transfer to combat duty, preferably aboard a destroyer."

ROBERTS. (*Tensely, going to* DOC.) That oughta do it, eh, Doc?

DOC. Doug, you've been sending in a letter every week for who knows how long . . .

ROBERTS. Not like this . . .

DOC. . . . and every week the Captain has screamed like a stuck pig, and forwarded your letters, "Disapproved."

ROBERTS. That's just my point, Doc. He *does* forward them. They go through the chain of command all the way back to Washington. . . . Just because the Captain doesn't . . .

DOC. Doug, the Captain of a Navy ship is the most absolute monarch left in this world!

ROBERTS. I know that.

DOC. If he endorsed your letter " approved " you'd get your orders in a minute . . .

ROBERTS. Naturally, but I . . . (*Turns away from* DOC.)

DOC. . . . but " disapproved," you haven't got a prayer. You're stuck on this old bucket, Doug. Face it!

ROBERTS. (*Turns quickly back.*) Well, grant me this much, Doc. That one day I'll find the perfect wording and one human guy will read those words and say, " Here's a poor son-of-a-bitch screaming for help. Let's put him on a fighting ship! "

DOC. (*Quietly.*) Sure . . .

ROBERTS. (*After a moment.*) I'm not kidding myself, am I, Doc? I've got a chance, haven't I?

DOC. Yes, Doug, you've got a chance. It's about the same chance as putting your letter in a bottle and dropping it in the ocean . . .

ROBERTS. (*Snatching letter from* DOC.) But it's still a chance, dammit! It's still a chance! (ROBERTS *stands looking out to sea.* DOC *watches him for a moment then speaks gently:*)

DOC. I wish to hell you'd never seen that task force. (*Pauses.*) Well, I've got to go down to my hypochondriacs. (*He goes off slowly through passageway.* ROBERTS *is still staring out as* DOWDY *enters from the hatchway. He is a hard-bitten man between thirty-five and forty and is wearing dungarees and no hat. He stands by hatchway with a cup of coffee in his hand.*)

DOWDY. 'Morning, Mister Roberts.

ROBERTS. Good morning, Dowdy.

DOWDY. Jeez, it's even hotter up here than down in that messhall! (*He looks off.*) Look at that cruddy island . . . smell it! Just like a hog pen. Think we'll get out of here today, sir? (ROBERTS *takes* DOWDY's *cup as he speaks and drinks from it, then hands it back.*)

ROBERTS. I don't know, Dowdy. There's one LCT coming alongside for supplies . . . (*Goes to hatchway, looks down.*) Are they getting up yet?

DOWDY. (*Also looking down hatch.*) Yeah, they're starting to stumble around down there—the poor punch-drunk bastards. Mister Roberts, when are you going to the Captain again and ask him to give this crew a liberty? These guys ain't been off the ship for over a year except on duty.

ROBERTS. Dowdy, the last time I asked him was last night.

DOWDY. What'd he say?

ROBERTS. He said " No."

DOWDY. We gotta get these guys ashore! They're going Asiatic! (*Pause.*)

ROBERTS. (*Hands* DOWDY *the letter.*) Have Dolan type that up for me. (*He starts off* R.)

DOWDY. (*Descending hatchway.*) Oh, your letter. Yes, sir! (ROBERTS *exits through passageway.* DOWDY *disappears down hatchway. He is heard below.*) All right, you guys in there. Finish your coffee and get up on deck. Stefanowski, Insigna, off your tails . . . (*After a moment the* C. *door opens and the* CAPTAIN *appears wearing pajamas and bathrobe and his officer's cap. He is carrying water in an engine-room oil can. He waters the palm tree carefully, looks at it for a moment tenderly and goes back into his cabin. After a moment,* DOWDY'S *voice is heard from the companionway and he appears followed by members of the crew.*) All right, let's go! (SCHLEMMER *exits by ladder to the bridge. Other men appear from the hatchway. They are* INSIGNA, STEFANOWSKI, MANNION, WILEY, REBER *and* LINDSTROM—*all yawning, buttoning pants, tucking in shirts and, in general, being comatose. The men do not appear to like one another very much at this hour—least of all* INSIGNA *and* MANNION.) All right, I got a little recreation for you guys. Stefanowski, you take these guys and get this little rust patch here. (*He hands* STEFANOWSKI *an armful of scrapers and wire brushes, indicating a spot on the deck.* STEFANOWSKI *looks at instruments dully, then distributes them to the men standing near him.* SCHLEMMER *returns from the bridge, carrying four pairs of binoculars and a spy glass. He drops them next to* INSIGNA *who is sitting on the hatch.*) Insigna, I got a real special job for you. You stay right here and clean these glasses.

INSIGNA. Ah, let me work up forward, Dowdy. I don't want to be around this crud, Mannion.

MANNION. Yeah, Dowdy. Take Insigna with you!

DOWDY. Shut up, I'm tired of you two bellyaching! (*Nodding to others to follow him.*) All right, guys, let's go. (DOWDY, REBER and SCHLEMMER *leave through passageway* R. *The others sit in sodden silence.* LINDSTROM *wanders slowly over to* INSIGNA. *He picks up spy glass and examines it. He holds the large end toward him and looks into it.*)

LINDSTROM. Hey, look! I can see myself!

STEFANOWSKI. Terrifying, ain't it? (INSIGNA *takes the spy glass from him and starts polishing it.* LINDSTROM *removes his shoe and feels inside it, then puts it back on.*)

MANNION. (*After a pause.*) Hey, what time is it in San Francisco?

INSIGNA. (*Scornfully.*) When?

MANNION. Anybody ask you? (*Turns to* WILEY.) What time would it be there, Wiley?

WILEY. I don't know. I guess about midnight last night.

MANNION. Midnight. San Francisco.

STEFANOWSKI. (*Studying scraper in his hand.*) I wonder if you could get sent back to the States if you cut off a finger. (*Nobody answers. Business.*)

INSIGNA. (*Looking offstage.*) Hey, they got a new building on that island. (*Nobody shows any curiosity.*)

MANNION. I had a girl in San Francisco wore flowers in her hair—instead of hats. Never wore a hat . . . (*Another sodden pause.*)

INSIGNA. (*Holding spy glass.*) Hey, Stefanowski! Which end of this you look through?

STEFANOWSKI. It's optional, Sam. Depends on what size eyeball you've got. (INSIGNA *idly looks through spy glass at something out* R. *Another pause.*)

INSIGNA. Hey, the Japs must've took over this island—there's a red and white flag on that new building.

MANNION. Japs! We never been within five thousand miles of a Jap! Japs! That's a hospital flag!

INSIGNA. Anybody ask you? (*Nudging* LINDSTROM *and pointing to the other group. Looks through spy glass.*) Hey, they got a fancy hospital . . . big windows and . . . (*Suddenly rises, gasping at what he sees.*)

STEFANOWSKI. What's the matter, Sam?

INSIGNA. She's—she's bare-assed!

STEFANOWSKI. *She!*

INSIGNA. Taking a shower . . . in that bathroom . . . that nurse . . . upstairs window! (*Instantly the others rush to hatch cover, grab binoculars and stand looking out* R.)

WILEY. She's a blonde—see!

LINDSTROM. I never seen such a beautiful girl!

MANNION. She's sure taking a long time in that shower!

WILEY. Yeah, honey, come on over here by the window!

INSIGNA. Don't you do it, honey! You take your own sweet time!

STEFANOWSKI. There's another one over by the washbasin—taking a shampoo.

INSIGNA. (*Indignantly.*) Yeah. But why the hell don't she take her bathrobe off! That's a stupid damn way to take a shampoo! (*For a moment the men watch in silent vigilance.*)

WILEY. She's coming out of the shower!

MANNION. She's coming over to the window! (*A pause.*) Kee-ri-mi-ny! (*For a moment the men stand transfixed, their faces radiant. They emit rapturous sighs. That is all.*)

LINDSTROM. Aw, she's turning around the other way!

MANNION. What's that red mark she's got . . . there?

INSIGNA. (*Authoritatively.*) That's a birthmark!

MANNION. (*Scornfully.*) Birthmark!

INSIGNA. What do you think it is, wise guy?

MANNION. Why, that's paint! She's sat in some red paint!

INSIGNA. Red paint! I'm tellin' you, that's a birthmark!

MANNION. Did you ever see a birthmark down there?

INSIGNA. (*Lowers his spy glass, turns to* MANNION.) Why, you stupid jerk! I had an uncle once had a birthmark right down . . .

WILEY. Aww! (INSIGNA *and* MANNION *return quickly to their glasses.*)

STEFANOWSKI. (*Groaning.*) She's put her bathrobe on! (*The four men notice something and exclaim in unison.*) They look exactly alike with those bathrobes on. Maybe they're twins.

MANNION. Yeah, but that's my gal on the right—the one with the red birthmark.

INSIGNA. You stupid crud, the one with the birthmark's on the left!

MANNION. The hell she is . . . (MANNION *and* INSIGNA *again lower their glasses.*)

INSIGNA. The hell she ain't . . .

WILEY. Awwww! (MANNION *and* INSIGNA *quickly drop their argument and look.*)

12

STEFANOWSKI. They're both leaving the bathroom together. . . . (*The men are dejected again.*)

LINDSTROM. Hey, there ain't no one in there now!

STEFANOWSKI. (*Lowering his glasses.*) Did you figure that out all by yourself? (*He looks through his glasses again.*)

MANNION. (*After a pause.*) Come on, girls, let's go!

WILEY. Yeah. Who's next to take a nice zippy shower?

INSIGNA. (*After a pause.*) They must think we got nothing better to do than stand here!

LINDSTROM. These glasses are getting heavy!

STEFANOWSKI. Let's take turns, okay? (*The others agree.*) Mannion, you take it first. (MANNION *nods, crosses and sits on bitt, keeping watch with his binoculars. The others pick up their scrapers and wire brushes.*)

INSIGNA. (*Watching* MANNION.) I don't trust that crud. (LINDSTROM *starts to sneak around front of hatch, holding his wire brush before his face.* STEFANOWSKI *hears a noise from the CAPTAIN's cabin and quickly warns the others.*)

STEFANOWSKI. Flash Red! (WILEY *repeats "Flash Red!" in a loud whisper. The men immediately begin working in earnest as the CAPTAIN, now in khaki, enters. He stands for a moment looking at them, and then wanders over to the group scraping the rust patch to inspect their work. Then, satisfied that they are actually working, he starts toward passageway. He sees MANNION, sitting on the bitt, looking through his glasses and smiling. The CAPTAIN goes over and stands beside him, looking off in the same direction.* STEFANOWSKI *tries frantically to signal a warning to MANNION by beating out code with his scraper.* MANNION *suddenly sees the CAPTAIN and quickly lowers his glasses and pretends to clean them, alternately wiping the lenses and holding them up to his eyes to see that they are clean. The CAPTAIN watches him suspiciously for a moment, then he exits by the ladder to the bridge.* STEFANOWSKI *rises and looks up ladder to make certain the CAPTAIN has gone.*) Flash White! (*He turns and looks at* MANNION.) Hey, Mannion. Anyone in there yet?

MANNION. (*Watching something happily through glasses.*) No, not yet!

INSIGNA. (*Picks up spy glass and looks, and rises quickly.*) Why, you dirty, miserable cheat! (*Instantly all the men are at the glasses.*)

LINDSTROM. There's one in there again!

STEFANOWSKI. The hell with her—she's already got her clothes on!

INSIGNA. And there she goes! (*Slowly lowers his glass, turning to* MANNION *threateningly.*) Why, you lousy, cheating crud!

MANNION. (*Idly swinging his glasses.*) That ain't all. I seen three!

STEFANOWSKI. You lowdown Peeping Tom!

LINDSTROM. (*Hurt.*) Mannion, that's a real dirty trick.

INSIGNA. What's the big idea?

MANNION. Who wants to know?

INSIGNA. I want to know! And you're damn well going to tell me!

MANNION. You loud-mouthed little bastard! Why don't you make me?

INSIGNA. You're damn right I will. Right now! (*He swings on* MANNION *as* LINDSTROM *steps clumsily between them.*)

LINDSTROM. Hey, fellows! Fellows!

INSIGNA. No wonder you ain't got a friend on this ship . . . except this crud, Wiley. (*He jerks his head in direction of* WILEY *who stands behind him on hatch cover.* WILEY *takes him by shoulder and whirls him around.*)

WILEY. What'd you say?

STEFANOWSKI. (*Shoving* WILEY.) You heard him! (MANNION *jumps on hatch cover to protect* WILEY *from* STEFANOWSKI. INSIGNA *rushes at* MANNION *and for a moment they are all in a clinch.* LINDSTROM *plows up on the hatch and breaks them apart. The men have suddenly formed into two camps—*MANNION *and* WILEY *on one side,* INSIGNA *and* STEFANOWSKI *facing them.* LINDSTROM *is just an accessory, but stands prepared to intervene if necessary.*)

MANNION. (*To* WILEY.) Look at them two! Everybody on the ship hates their guts! The two moochingest, no-good loud-mouths on the ship! (STEFANOWSKI *starts for* MANNION *but* INSIGNA *pulls him back and steps menacingly toward* MANNION.)

INSIGNA. Why, you slimy, lying son-of-a-bitch! (*Suddenly* MANNION *hits* INSIGNA, *knocking him down. He jumps on* INSIGNA *who catches* MANNION *in the chest with his feet and hurls him back.* WILEY *and* STEFANOWSKI *start fighting with* LINDSTROM, *attempting to break them apart.* MANNION *rushes back at* INSIGNA. INSIGNA *sidesteps* MANNION'S *lunge and knocks him to the deck.* INSIGNA *falls on him. They wrestle to their feet and stand slugging. At this point* ROBERTS *and* DOWDY *run on from passageway.* ROBERTS *flings* INSIGNA *and* MANNION *apart.* DOWDY *separates the others.*)

14

ROBERTS. Break it up! Break it up, I tell you! (INSIGNA *and* MAN-NION *rush at each other.* ROBERTS *and* DOWDY *stop them.*)

DOWDY. O. K., you guys, break it up!

ROBERTS. All right! What's going on?

INSIGNA. (*Pointing at* MANNION.) This son-of-a-bitch here . . .

ROBERTS. Did you hear me?

MANNION. (*To* INSIGNA.) Shut your mouth!

DOWDY. Shut up, both of you!

INSIGNA. Slimy son-of-a-bitch! (*Picks up scraper and lunges at* MANNION *again.* ROBERTS *throws him back.*)

ROBERTS. I said to cut it out! Did you hear me? (*Wheels on* MAN-NION.) That goes for you too! (*Includes entire group. The men stand subdued, breathing hard from the fight.*) Now get to work! All of you! (*They begin to move sullenly off* R.) Mannion, you and the rest get to work beside number two! And, Insigna, take those glasses way up to the bow and work on them! Stefanowski, keep those two apart.

STEFANOWSKI. Yes, sir. (*The men exit.* ROBERTS *and* DOWDY *look after them.*)

DOWDY. (*Tightly.*) They've got to have a liberty, Mister Roberts.

ROBERTS. They sure do. Dowdy, call a boat for me, will you? I'm going ashore.

DOWDY. What are you going to do?

ROBERTS. I just got a new angle.

DOWDY. Are you going over the Captain's head?

ROBERTS. No, I'm going around his end—I hope. Get the lead out, Dowdy. (*He exits* L. *as* DOWDY *goes off* R. *and the lights*)

FADE OUT

(*During the darkness, voices can be heard over the squawk-box saying:*)

Now hear this . . . now hear this. Sweepers, man your brooms. Clean sweep-down fore and aft. Sweep-down all ladders and all passageways. Do *not* throw trash over the fantail.

Now, all men on report will see the master-at-arms for assignment to extra duty.

Now hear this . . . now hear this. Because in violation of the Captain's orders, a man has appeared on deck without a shirt on, there will be no movies again tonight—by order of the Captain.

15

SCENE 2

The lights dim up revealing the stateroom of PULVER
and ROBERTS. *Two lockers are shown, one marked " Ensign F. J. Pulver," the other marked " Lt. (jg) D. A.
Roberts." There is a double bunk along the bulkhead* R.
A desk with its end against the bulkhead L. *has a chair
at either side. There is a porthole in the bulkhead above
it. Up* C., R. *of* PULVER'S *locker is a washbasin over
which is a shelf and a medicine chest. The door is up* C.
An officer is discovered with his head inside ROBERTS'
*locker, throwing skivvy shirts over his shoulder as he
searches for something.* DOLAN, *a young, garrulous, brash
yeoman, second class, enters. He is carrying a file folder.*

DOLAN. Here's your letter, Mister Roberts. (*He goes to the desk,
taking fountain pen from his pocket.*) I typed it up. Just sign your
old John Henry here and I'll take it in to the Captain . . . then
hold your ears. (*No answer.*) Mister Roberts! (PULVER'S *head
appears from the locker.*) Oh, it's only you, Mister Pulver. What
are you doing in Mister Roberts' locker?

PULVER. (*Hoarsely.*) Dolan, I know there's a shoe box in there,
but I can't find it. (DOLAN *looks in the locker.*) They've stolen that
shoe box! There's nothing they'll stop at now. They've broken
right into the sanctity of a man's own locker. (*He sits in chair at
desk.*)

DOLAN. (*Disinterested.*) Ain't Mister Roberts back from the island
yet?

PULVER. No.

DOLAN. Well, as soon as he gets back, will you ask him to sign
this baby?

PULVER. What is it?

DOLAN. What is it! It's the best damn letter Mister Roberts writ
yet. It's going to blow the Old Man right through the overhead.
And them big shots in Washington are going to drop their drawers
too. This letter is liable to get him transferred.

PULVER. Yeah, lemme see it.

DOLAN. (*Handing letter to* PULVER.) Get a load of that last para-
graph.

PULVER. Where?

DOLAN. Right here.

PULVER. (*Reading with apprehension.*) ". . . increase disharmony aboard this ship . . ."

DOLAN. (*Interrupting gleefully.*) Won't that frost the Old Man's knockers? I can't wait to jab this baby in the Old Man's face. Mister Pulver, you know how he gets sick to his stomach when he gets extra mad at Mister Roberts—well, when I deliver this letter I'm going to take along a wastebasket! Let me know when Mister Roberts gets back. (DOLAN *exits.* PULVER *continues reading the letter with great dismay. He hears* ROBERTS *and* DOC *talking in the passageway, offstage, and quickly goes to his bunk and hides the letter under a blanket. He goes to the locker and is replacing skivvy shirts as* ROBERTS *and* DOC *enter.*)

ROBERTS. . . . so after the fight I figured I had to do something and do it quick! (*Sitting in chair and searching through desk drawer.*) Hey, Frank, has Dolan been in here yet with my letter?

PULVER. (*Innocently.*) I don't know, Doug boy. I just came in here myself.

DOC. You don't know anybody on the island, do you, Doug?

ROBERTS. Yes. The Port Director—the guy who decides where to send this ship next. A Liberty Port, for instance. He confided to me that he used to drink a quart of whiskey every day of his life. So this morning when I broke up that fight it came to me that he might just possibly sell his soul for a quart of Scotch.

PULVER. (*Rises.*) Doug, you didn't give that shoe box to the Port Director!

ROBERTS. I did. " Compliments of the Captain."

DOC. You've been hoarding a quart of Scotch in a shoe box?

ROBERTS. Johnny Walker! I was going to break it out the day I got off this ship—Resurrection Day!

PULVER. Then —— It's really gone! (*He sinks to the bunk.*)

DOC. Well, did the Port Director say he'd send us to a Liberty Port?

ROBERTS. Hell, no. He took the Scotch and said, " Don't bother me, Roberts. I'm busy." The boozer!

PULVER. How could you do it!

DOC. Well, where there's a boozer, there's hope. Maybe when he gets working on that Scotch he'll mellow a little.

PULVER. Douglas Roberts, you wasted that bottle on some damn man!

ROBERTS. Man! Will you name me another sex within a thousand miles . . . (PULVER, *dejected, goes up to porthole.*) What the hell's eating you anyhow, Frank? (DOC *crosses to bunk. He sees two fancy pillows on bottom bunk, picks up one and tosses it to* ROBERTS. *He picks up the other.*)

DOC. Well, look at the fancy pillows. Somebody seems to be expecting company!

ROBERTS. Good Lord!

DOC. (*Reads lettering on pillowcase.*) "Toujours l'amour . . . Souvenir of San Diego . . . Oo-la-la!

ROBERTS. (*Reading from his pillowcase.*) "Tonight or never . . . Compliments of Allis-Chalmers, Farm Equipment . . . We plow deep while others sleep." (*He looks at* DOC, *then rises.*) Doc—that new hospital over there hasn't got nurses, has it?

DOC. Nurses! It didn't have yesterday!

PULVER. (*Turning from porthole.*) It has today!

DOC. But how did you find out they were there?

PULVER. (*Trying to recall.*) Now let me think . . . it just came to me all of a sudden. This morning I was just lying on my bunk—thinking . . . There wasn't a breath of air. And then, all of a sudden, a little breeze came up and I took a big deep breath and said to myself, "Pulver boy, there's women on that there island."

ROBERTS. Doc, a thing like this could make a bird dog self-conscious as hell.

PULVER. (*Warming up.*) Eighteen of them transferred in last night —all brunettes except for two beautiful blondes—twin sisters! I'm working on one of those. I asked her out to the ship for lunch, but she said no. So I turned on the old personality—I said, "Ain't there anything in the world that'll make you come out to the ship with me?" And she said, "Yes, there is, one thing and one thing only"—(*Crosses to* ROBERTS, *looks at him accusingly*) "a good stiff drink of Scotch!" (*He sinks into the chair.*)

ROBERTS. (*After a pause.*) I'm sorry, Frank.

PULVER. Yeah, you're sorry.

ROBERTS. No, I'm really sorry. Your first assignment in a year. (*He pats* PULVER *on the shoulder.*)

PULVER. I figured I'd bring her in here . . . I got out my old pillows . . . (*Fondling pillow on desk.*) and then I was going to throw a couple of fast slugs of Scotch into her and . . . but, hell, without the Scotch, she wouldn't . . . she just wouldn't, that's all.

ROBERTS. (*After a pause.*) Doc, let's make some Scotch!

DOC. Huh?

ROBERTS. As naval officers we're supposed to be resourceful. Frank here's got a great opportunity and I've let him down. Let's fix him up!

DOC. Right! (*He goes to desk.* ROBERTS *begins removing bottles from medicine chest.*) Frank, where's the rest of that alcohol we were drinking last night?

PULVER. (*Pulling a large vinegar bottle half filled with colorless liquid from the wastebasket and handing it to* DOC.) Hell, that ain't even the right color.

DOC. (*Taking the bottle.*) Quiet! (*Thinks deeply.*) Color . . . (*With sudden decision.*) Coca-Cola! Have you got any?

ROBERTS. I haven't seen a Coke in four months—no, by golly, it's five months!

PULVER. Oh, what the hell! (*He rises, crosses to bunk, reaches under mattress of top bunk and produces a bottle of Coca-Cola. The others watch him.* DOC *snatches the bottle.* PULVER *says apologetically.*) I forgot I had it. (DOC *opens the bottle and is about to pour the Coca-Cola into the vinegar bottle when he suddenly stops.*)

DOC. Oh—what shade would you like?

PULVER. Shade?

DOC. . . . Light or Dark? Cutty Sark.

ROBERTS. Vat 69?

PULVER. (*Interested.*) I told her Johnny Walker.

DOC. Johnny Walker it is! (*He pours some of the Coca-Cola into the bottle.*)

ROBERTS. (*Looking at color of the mixture.*) Red Label!

DOC. Red Label!

PULVER. It may look like it—but it sure as hell won't taste like it!

ROBERTS. Doc, what does Scotch taste like?

DOC. Er . . .

ROBERTS. Do you know what it's always tasted a little like to me? Iodine.

DOC. (*Shrugs as if to say "Of course" and rises. He takes dropper from small bottle of iodine and flicks a drop in the bottle.*) One drop of iodine—for taste. (*Shakes the bottle and pours some in glass.*)

PULVER. Lemme taste her, Doc!

DOC. (*Stops him with a gesture.*) No. This calls for a medical

19

opinion. (*Takes a ceremonial taste while the others wait for his verdict.*)

PULVER. How about it?

DOC. We're on the right track! (*Sets glass down. Rubs hands professionally.*) Now we need a little something extra—for age! What've you got there, Doug?

ROBERTS. (*Reading labels of bottles on desk.*) Bromo-Seltzer . . . Eno Fruit Salts . . . Kreml Hair Tonic . . .

DOC. Kreml! It has a coal-tar base! And it'll age the hell out of it! (*Pours a bit of Kreml into mixture. Shakes bottle solemnly.*) One drop Kreml for age. (*Sets bottle on desk, looks at wrist watch for a fraction of a second.*) That's it! (*Pours drink into glass. PULVER reaches for it. ROBERTS pushes his arm aside and tastes it.*)

ROBERTS. By golly, it does taste a little like Scotch! (*PULVER again reaches for glass. DOC pushes his arm aside and takes a drink.*)

DOC. By golly, it does! (*PULVER finally gets glass and takes a quick sip.*)

PULVER. Smooth —— That dumb little blonde won't know the difference.

DOC. (*Hands the bottle to PULVER.*) Here you are, Frank. Doug and I have made the Scotch. The *nurse* is your department. (*PULVER takes the bottle and hides it under the mattress, then replaces the pillows.*)

PULVER. (*Singing softly.*) Won't know the difference . . . won't know the difference. (*DOC starts to drink from Coca-Cola bottle as PULVER comes over and snatches it from his hand.*) Thanks, Doc. You won't know the difference, will you, honey? No, you won't—you sure as hell won't. (*Puts cap on the bottle and hides it under the mattress. Turns and faces the others.*) Thanks, Doug. Jeez, you guys are wonderful to me.

ROBERTS. (*Putting bottles back in medicine chest.*) Don't mention it, Frank. I think you almost deserve it.

PULVER. You do—really? Or are you just giving me the old needle again? What do you really think of me, Doug—honestly?

ROBERTS. (*Turning slowly to face PULVER.*) Frank, I like you. No one can get around the fact that you're a hell of a likeable guy.

PULVER. (*Beaming.*) Yeah—yeah . . .

ROBERTS. But . . .

PULVER. But what?

ROBERTS. But I also think you are the most hapless . . . lazy . . . disorganized . . . and, in general, the most lecherous person I've ever known in my life.

PULVER. I am not.

ROBERTS. Not what?

PULVER. I'm not disorganized—for one thing.

ROBERTS. Have you ever in your life finished anything you started out to do? You sleep sixteen hours a day. You pretend you want me to improve your mind and you've never even finished one book I've given you to read!

PULVER. I finished *God's Little Acre*, Doug boy!

ROBERTS. I didn't give you that! (*To* DOC.) He's been reading *God's Little Acre* for over a year! (*Takes dog-eared book from* PULVER's *bunk.*) He's underlined every erotic passage, and added exclamation points—and after a certain pornographic climax, he's inserted the words "damn well written." (*To* PULVER.) You're the Laundry and Morale Officer and I doubt if you've ever seen the Laundry.

PULVER. I was down there only last week.

ROBERTS. And you're scared of the Captain.

PULVER. I'm not scared of the Captain.

ROBERTS. Then why do you hide in the passageway every time you see him coming? I doubt if he even knows you're on board. You're scared of him.

PULVER. I am not. I'm scared of myself—I'm scared of what *I* might do to him.

ROBERTS. (*Laughing.*) What you might do to him! Doc, he lies in his sack all day long and bores me silly with great moronic plots against the Captain and he's never carried out one.

PULVER. I haven't, huh.

ROBERTS. No, Frank, you haven't. What ever happened to your idea of plugging up the line of the Captain's sanitary system? "I'll make it overflow," you said. "I'll make a backwash that'll lift him off the throne and knock him clean across the room."

PULVER. I'm workin' on that. I thought about it for half an hour —just yesterday.

ROBERTS. Half an hour!

PULVER. Yeah, I thought about it for half an hour just yesterday.

ROBERTS. He's gonna give up. There's only one thing you've thought about for half an hour in your life! And what about those marbles that you were going to put in the Captain's overhead—so they'd roll around at night and keep him awake?

PULVER. Now you've gone too far. Now you've asked for it. (*Goes to bunk and produces small tin box from under mattress. Crosses to* ROBERTS *and shakes it in his face. Opens it.*) What does that look like? Five marbles! And I've got one right here in my pocket! (*Takes marble from pocket, holds it close to* ROBERTS' *nose, then drops it in box. Closes box.*) Six marbles! (*Puts box back under mattress, turns defiantly to* ROBERTS.) I'm looking for marbles all day long!

ROBERTS. Frank, you asked me what I thought of you. Well, I'll tell you! The day you finish one thing you've started out to do, the day you actually put those marbles in the Captain's overhead, and then have the guts to knock on his door and say, " Captain, I put those marbles there," that's the day I'll have some respect for you—that's the day I'll look up to you as a man. Okay?

PULVER. (*Belligerently.*) Okay! (ROBERTS *goes to the radio and turns it up. While he is listening,* DOC *and* PULVER *exchange worried looks.*)

RADIO VOICE. . . . intersecting thirty miles north of Hanover. The abrupt German collapse brought forth the remark from a high London official that the end of the war in Europe is only weeks away—maybe days . . . (ROBERTS *turns off radio.*)

ROBERTS. Where the hell's Dolan with that letter! (*Starts toward the door.*) I'm going to find him.

PULVER. Hey, Doug, wait! Listen! (ROBERTS *pauses at the door.*) I wouldn't send in that letter if I were you!

ROBERTS. What do you mean—*that* letter!

PULVER. (*Hastily.*) I mean any of those letters you been writin'. What are you so nervous about anyway?

ROBERTS. Nervous!

PULVER. I mean about getting off this ship. We're a threesome, aren't we—you and Doc and me? Share and share alike! You didn't think I was going to keep those nurses all to myself. Soon as I get my little nursie under control, I'm going to start working on her twin sister—for you.

22

ROBERTS. That's damn decent of you, Frank.

PULVER. And then I'm going to scare up something for you too, Doc. And in the meantime you've got a lot of work to do, Doug boy—improvin' my mind and watching my grammar. And speaking of grammar, you better watch your grammar. You're going to get in trouble, saying things like "disharmony aboard this ship!" (ROBERTS *looks at* PULVER *quickly.* PULVER *catches himself.*) I mean just in case you ever said anything like "disharmony aboard this ship" . . . or . . . uh . . . "harmony aboard this ship" or . . .

ROBERTS. Where's that letter?

PULVER. (*Shouting.*) I don't know, Doug boy . . . (*As* ROBERTS *steps toward him, he quickly produces the letter from the blanket.*) Here it is, Doug.

ROBERTS. (*Snatching the letter.*) What's the big idea! (ROBERTS *goes to desk, reading and preparing to sign the letter.* PULVER *follows him.*)

PULVER. I just wanted to talk to you before you signed it. You can't send it in that way—it's too strong! Don't sign that letter, Doug, please don't! They'll transfer you and you'll get your ass shot off. You're just running a race with death, isn't he, Doc? It's stupid to keep asking for it like that. The Doc says so too. Tell him what you said to me last night, Doc—about how stupid he is.

ROBERTS. (*Coldly, to* DOC.) Yes, Doc, maybe you'd like to tell me to my face.

DOC. (*Belligerently.*) Yes, I would. Last night I asked you why you wanted to fight this war. And you said: anyone who doesn't fight it is only half-alive. Well, I thought that over and I've decided that's just a crockful, Doug—just a crockful.

ROBERTS. I take it back, Doc. After seeing that task force I don't feel that much alive.

DOC. You are stupid! And I can prove it! You quit medical school to get into this thing when you could be saving lives today. Why? Do you even know yourself?

ROBERTS. Has it ever occurred to you that the guys who fight this war might also be saving lives . . . yours and mine, for instance! Not just putting men together again, but *keeping* them together! Right now I'd rather practice that kind of medicine—Doctor!

DOC. (*Rising.*) Well, right now, that's exactly what you're doing.

ROBERTS. What!

DOC. Whether you like it or not, this sorry old bucket does a necessary job.

ROBERTS. This sorry old bucket does a necessary job.

DOC. And you're the guy who keeps her lumbering along. You keep this crew working cargo, and more than that—you keep them *alive*. It might just be that right here, on this bucket, you're deeper and more truly in this war than you ever would be anywhere else.

ROBERTS. Oh, geez, Doc. In a minute, you'll start quoting Emerson.

DOC. *That* is a lousy thing to say!

ROBERTS. We've got nothing to do with the war. Maybe that's why we're on this ship—because we're not good enough to fight. (*Then quietly with emotion.*) Maybe there's some omniscient son-of a bitch who goes down the line of all the servicemen and picks out the ones to send into combat, the ones whose glands secrete enough adrenalin, or whose great-great-grandfathers weren't afraid of the dark or something. The rest of us are shoved off to ships like this where we can't do any harm.

DOC. What is it you want to be—a hero or something?

ROBERTS. (*Shocked.*) Doc! Look, Doc, the war's way out there! I'm here. I don't want to be here—I want to be out there. I'm sick and tired of being a lousy spectator. I've got to feel I'm *good* enough to be in this thing—to *participate!*

DOC. Good enough! Doug, you're good enough! You just don't have the opportunity. That's mostly what physical heroism is— opportunity. It's a reflex. I think seventy-five out of a hundred young males have that reflex. If you put any one of them—say, even Frank Thurlowe Pulver, here—in a B-29 over Japan, do you know what you'd have?

ROBERTS. No, I don't, Doctor.

DOC. You'd have Pulver, the Congressional Medal of Honor winner! You'd have Pulver, who, singlehanded, shot down twenty-three attacking Japanese planes, Pulver who with his bare hands held together the severed wing struts of his plane, and with his bare feet successfully landed the mortally wounded plane on his home field. (PULVER *thinks this over.*) Hell, it's a reflex. It's like the knee jerk. Strike the patella tendon of any human being and you produce the knee jerk. Look. (*He illustrates on* PULVER. *There is no knee jerk. He strikes again—still no reaction.*)

24

PULVER. What's the matter, Doc?

DOC. Nothing. But stay out of B-29's, Frank, my boy.

ROBERTS. You've made your point very vividly, Doc. But I'm figuring to get into this thing. And I'm going to keep on sending in these letters until I do. (ROBERTS *signs the letter. Then to* DOC.) I haven't got much time. That task force is on its way to start our last big push against the Japanese. And it went by me, Doc. I plan to catch it. (*He exits.*)

PULVER. I'm gonna show him he's got old Pulver figured out all wrong. (*Pulls small cardboard roll from under mattress.*) Doc, what does that look like?

DOC. Just what it is—the cardboard center of a roll of toilet paper.

PULVER. I suppose it doesn't look like a firecracker.

DOC. Not a bit like a firecracker.

PULVER. (*Taking a piece of string from the bunk.*) I suppose that doesn't look like a fuse. Well, you just wait till old Pulver gets through with it. (DOC *rises and starts off. He walks slowly out of the room.* PULVER *goes on.*) I'm going to get me some of that black powder from the gunner's mate. No, sir, see, sir, this isn't going to be any peanut firecracker—I'm going to get some of that stuff they use to blow up bridges, that fulminate of mercury stuff. An' then on the night of Doug's birthday I'm going to throw it under the Old Man's bunk. Bam—bam—bam! (*Knocks on* ROBERTS' *locker, opens it.*) Captain, it is I, Ensign Pulver. I just threw that firecracker under your stinking damn bunk. (*He salutes as the lights*)

FADE OUT

(*In the darkness we hear the sound of a winch and shouted orders:*)

LCT OFFICER. On the AK—where do you want us?

AK VOICE. Starboard side, up for'd—alongside number two!

LCT OFFICER. Shall we use our fenders or yours?

AK VOICE. No, we'll use ours! Stand off till we finish with the barge!

SCENE 3

The curtain rises and the lights dim up on the deck. ROBERTS *stands on the hatch cover.* SCHLEMMER, GER-

25

HART *and another seaman are sitting on the hatch cover.
They are tired and hot. A cargo net, filled with crates,
is disappearing off* R. *Offstage we hear the shouts of men
working cargo. Two officers walk across the stage.
Everyone's shirt is wet with perspiration.*

ROBERTS. (*Calling through megaphone.*) Okay—take it away—
that's all for the barge. On the LCT—I'll give you a bow line.

LCT OFFICER. (*Offstage.*) Okay, Lieutenant.

ROBERTS. (*To crew.*) Get a line over!

DOWDY. (*Offstage.*) Yes, sir!

REBER. (*Off* R.) Heads up on the LCT!

ROBERTS. That's good. Make it fast. (PAYNE, *wearing the belt of
a messenger, enters from companionway as* DOWDY *enters from* R.)

PAYNE. Mister Roberts, the Captain says not to give this LCT any
fresh fruit. He says he's going to keep what's left for his own mess.

ROBERTS. Okay, okay . . .

PAYNE. Hold your hat, Mister Roberts. I just saw Dolan go in
there with your letter. (*He grins and exits as* ROBERTS *smiles at*
DOWDY.)

DOWDY. Here's the list of what the LCT guy wants.

ROBERTS. (*Reading rapidly.*) One ton dry stores . . . quarter-ton
frozen food . . . one gross dungarees . . . Okay, we can give
him all that.

DOWDY. Can these guys take their shirts off while we're working?

ROBERTS. Dowdy, you know the Captain has a standing order . . .

DOWDY. One guy just passed out from the heat.

ROBERTS. (*Looks at men who wait for his decision.*) Hell, yes,
take 'em off. (DOWDY *exits.* SCHLEMMER, REBER *and seaman remove shirts saying " Thanks, Mister Roberts" and exit* R. ROBERTS
calls through megaphone.) LCT, want to swap movies? We've got
a new one.

LCT. (*Offstage.*) What's that?

ROBERTS. Hoot Gibson in *Riders of the Range.*

LCT. (*Offstage.*) No, thanks, we've seen that three times!

DOWDY. (*Entering from* R.) All set, Mister Roberts.

LCT. (*Offstage.*) Lieutenant, one thing I didn't put on my list because I wanted to ask you—you couldn't spare us any fresh fruit,
could you?

ROBERTS. You all out?

LCT. (*Offstage.*) We haven't seen any for two months.

ROBERTS. (*To* DOWDY.) Dowdy, give 'em a couple of crates of oranges.

DOWDY. Yes, sir.

ROBERTS. Compliments of the Captain.

DOWDY. Aye-aye, sir. (*He exits.*)

ROBERTS. (*To* LCT.) Here comes your first sling-load! (*There is the grinding sound of a winch. With hand-signals* ROBERTS *directs placing of the sling-load. Then he shouts:*) Watch that line! (DOWDY'S *voice is heard offstage:*)

DOWDY. Slack off, you dumb bastards! Slack off! (PAYNE *enters.* ROBERTS *turns to him sharply.*)

ROBERTS. What!

PAYNE. The Captain wants to see you, Mister Roberts.

DOWDY. (*Offstage.*) Dammit, there it goes! You've parted the line!

ROBERTS. Get a fender over! Quick! (*To* PAYNE.) You go tell the Captain I'm busy! (PAYNE *exits.* ROBERTS *calls offstage.*) Get a line over—his bow's coming in!

REBER. (*Offstage.*) Heads up!

GERHART. (*Offstage.*) Where shall we secure?

DOWDY. (*Offstage.*) Secure here!

ROBERTS. No. Take it around the bitt!

DOWDY. (*Offstage.*) Around the bitt!

ROBERTS. That's too much! Give him some slack this time! (*Watches intently.*) That's good. Okay. Secure.

DOWDY. All secure. Let's give him the rest of his cargo.

GERHART. (*Entering quickly and pointing toward companionway.*) Flash Red! (*He exits. The* CAPTAIN *enters, followed by* PAYNE *and* DOLAN.)

CAPTAIN. All right, Mister! Let's have this out right here and now! What do you mean—telling me you're busy!

ROBERTS. We parted a line, Captain. You didn't want me to leave the deck with this ship coming in on us?

CAPTAIN. You're damn right I want you to leave the deck. When I tell you I want to see you, I mean *now*, Mister! I mean jump! Do you understand? (*At this point a group of men, attracted by the noise, crowd in. They are naked to the waist. They pretend they are working, but actually they are listening to the* CAPTAIN'S *fight with* ROBERTS.)

ROBERTS. Yes, Captain. I'll remember that next time.

CAPTAIN. You're damn right you'll remember it! Don't *ever* tell me you're too busy to see me! Ever! (ROBERTS *doesn't answer. The* CAPTAIN *points to the letter he is carrying.*) You think you're pretty cute with this letter, don't you? You're trying to get me in bad with the Admiral, ain't you? Ain't you?

ROBERTS. No, I'm not, Captain.

CAPTAIN. Then what do you mean by writing " disharmony aboard this ship "?

ROBERTS. Because it's true, Captain. (*The men grin at each other.*)

CAPTAIN. Any disharmony on this ship is my own doing!

ROBERTS. That's true too, Captain.

CAPTAIN. Damn right it's true. And it ain't gonna be in any letter that leaves this ship. Any criticism of this ship stays on this ship. I got a reputation with the Admiral and I ain't gonna lose it on account of a letter written by some smart-alec college officer. Now you retype that letter and leave out that disharmony crap and I'll send it in. But this is the last one, understand?

ROBERTS. Captain, every man in the Navy has the right to send in a request for transfer . . . and no one can change the wording. That's in Navy regs.

CAPTAIN. (*After a pause.*) How about that, Dolan?

DOLAN. That's what it says, sir.

CAPTAIN. This sons-a-bitchin' Navy! I never put up with crap like that in the merchant service. All right, I'll send this one in as it is— disapproved, like I always do. But there's one thing I don't have to do and that's send in a letter that ain't been written. And, Mister, I'm tellin' you here and now—you ain't gonna write any more. You bring one next week and you'll regret it the rest of your life. You got a job right here and, Mister, you ain't *never* going to leave this ship. Now get on with your work. (*He looks around and notices the men. He shouts.*) Where are your shirts?

ROBERTS. Captain, I . . .

CAPTAIN. Shut up! *Answer me, where are your shirts?* (*They stare at him.*) Get those shirts on in a damn quick hurry. (*The men pick up their shirts, then pause, looking at* ROBERTS.)

ROBERTS. Captain, it was so hot working cargo, I . . .

CAPTAIN. (*Shouting louder.*) I told you to shut up! (*To the men.*) I'm giving you an order: get those shirts on! (*The men do not move.*)

28

ROBERTS. (*Quietly.*) I'm sorry. Put your shirts on. (*The men put on their shirts. There is a pause while the* CAPTAIN *stares at the men. Then he speaks quietly:*)

CAPTAIN. Who's the Captain of this ship? That's the rankest piece of insubordination I've seen. You've been getting pretty smart playing grab-ass with Roberts here . . . but now you've gone too far. I'm givin' you a little promise—I ain't never gonna forget this. And in the meantime, every one of you men who disobeyed my standing order and appeared on deck without a shirt—every one—is on report, do you hear? On report!

ROBERTS. Captain, you're not putting these men on report.

CAPTAIN. What do you mean—I'm not!

ROBERTS. I'm responsible. I gave them permission.

CAPTAIN. You disobeyed my order?

ROBERTS. Yes, sir. It was too hot working cargo in the sun. One man passed out.

CAPTAIN. I don't give a damn if fifty men passed out. I gave an order and you disobeyed it.

LCT. (*Offstage.*) Thanks a million for the oranges, Lieutenant.

CAPTAIN. (*To* ROBERTS.) Did you give that LCT fresh fruit?

ROBERTS. Yes, sir. We've got plenty, Captain They've been out for two months.

CAPTAIN. I've taken all the crap from you that I'm going to. You've just got yourself ten days in your room. Ten days, Mister! Ten days!

ROBERTS. Very well, Captain. Do you relieve me here?

CAPTAIN. You're damn right, I relieve you. You can go to your room for ten days! See how you like that!

LCT. (*Offstage.*) We're waiting on you, Lieutenant. We gotta shove off. (ROBERTS *gives the megaphone to the* CAPTAIN *and starts off. The* CAPTAIN *looks in direction of the* LCT *then calls to* ROBERTS.)

CAPTAIN. Where do you think you're going?

ROBERTS. (*Pretending surprise.*) To my room, Captain!

CAPTAIN. Get back to that cargo! I'll let you know when you have ten days in your room and you'll damn well know it! You're going to stay right here and do your job! (ROBERTS *crosses to the crew. The* CAPTAIN *slams the megaphone into* ROBERTS' *stomach.* PULVER *enters around the corner of the house, sees the*

CAPTAIN *and starts to go back. The* CAPTAIN *sees* PULVER *and shouts:)* Who's that? Who's that officer there?

PULVER. *(Turning.)* Me, sir?

CAPTAIN. Yes, you. Come here, boy. (PULVER *approaches in great confusion and can think of nothing better to do than salute. This visibly startles the* CAPTAIN.) Why, you're one of my officers!

PULVER. Yes, sir.

CAPTAIN. What's your name again?

PULVER. Ensign Pulver, sir. *(He salutes again. The* CAPTAIN, *amazed, returns the salute, then says for the benefit of* ROBERTS *and the crew:)*

CAPTAIN. I'm glad to see one on this ship knows how to salute. *(Then to* PULVER.) Pulver . . . oh, yes . . . Pulver. How is it I never see you around?

PULVER. *(Terrified.)* I've wondered about that myself, sir.

CAPTAIN. What's your job?

PULVER. *(Trembling.)* Officer in charge of laundry and morale, sir.

CAPTAIN. How long you been aboard?

PULVER. Fourteen months, sir.

CAPTAIN. Fourteen months! You spend most of your time down in the laundry, eh?

PULVER. Most of the time, sir. Yes, sir. (ROBERTS *turns his face to hide his laughter.)*

CAPTAIN. Well, you do a good job, Pulver, and . . . you know I'd like to see more of you. Why don't you have lunch with me in my cabin today?

PULVER. Oh, I can't today.

CAPTAIN. Can't? Why not?

PULVER. I'm on my way over to the hospital on the island. I've got to go pick up a piece . . . of medical equipment.

ROBERTS. *(Calling over.)* Why, I'll take care of that, Frank.

CAPTAIN. That's right, Roberts. You finish here and you go over and fetch it.

ROBERTS. Yes, sir. *(He nods and turns away grinning.)*

CAPTAIN. *(To* PULVER.) Well, how about it?

PULVER. This is something I wouldn't want anyone else to do for me, sir.

CAPTAIN. Well, some other time then.

PULVER. Yes, sir. Thank you, sir.

CAPTAIN. Okay, Pulver. (*The* CAPTAIN *baits another salute from* PULVER, *then exits.* PULVER *watches him go, then starts to sneak off.*)

ROBERTS. (*Grinning and mimicking the* CAPTAIN.) Oh, boy! (PULVER *stops uneasily.* ROBERTS *salutes him.*) I want to see more of you, Pulver!

PULVER. (*Furiously.*) That blind old son-of-a-bitch! Pretending he doesn't know me! (*He looks at watch and exits.* ROBERTS *turns laughing to the crew who are standing rather solemnly.*)

DOWDY. (*Quietly.*) Nice going, Mister Roberts.

SCHLEMMER. It was really beautiful the way you read the Old Man off!

GERHART. Are you going to send in that letter next week, Mister Roberts?

ROBERTS. Are we, Dolan?

DOLAN. You're damn right we are! And I'm the baby who's going to deliver it!

SCHLEMMER. He said he'd fix you good. What do you think he'll do?

REBER. You got a promotion coming up, haven't you?

SCHLEMMER. Yeah. Could he stop that or something?

DOLAN. Promotion! This is Mister Roberts. You think he gives a good hoot-in-hell about another lousy stripe?

ALL. Yeah.

GERHART. Hey, Mister Roberts, can I take the letter in next week?

DOLAN. (*Indignantly.*) You can like hell! That's my job—isn't it, Mister Roberts?

GERHART. Can I, Mister Roberts?

ROBERTS. I'm afraid I've promised that job to Dolan.

DOLAN. (*Pushing* GERHART *away.*) You heard him. (*To* ROBERTS.) We gotta write a really hot one next week.

ROBERTS. Got any asbestos paper? All right, let's give him the rest of his cargo. (*He starts off, the men follow happily as the lights*)

FADE OUT

SCENE 4

The lights come up immediately on the main set. REBER *and* GERHART *enter from* R. *passageway. As they get*

31

around the corner of the house, they break into a run
REBER *dashes off through* L. *passageway.*

GERHART. (*Excitedly, descending hatchway.*) Hey, Schlemmer! Schlemmer! (MISS GIRARD, *a young, attractive, blond Army nurse, and* PULVER *enter from* R. *passageway.*)
PULVER. Well, here it is.
MISS GIRARD. This is a ship?
PULVER. Unh-hunh.
MISS GIRARD. My sister and I flew over some warships on our way out from the States and they looked so busy—men running around like mad.
PULVER. It's kinda busy sometimes up on deck.
MISS GIRARD. Oh, you mean you've had a lot of action?
PULVER. Well, I sure as hell haven't had much in the last year . . . Oh, battle action! Yeah . . . Yeah . . .
MISS GIRARD. Then you must have a lot of B. F. on here.
PULVER. Hunh?
MISS GIRARD. You know—battle fatigue?
PULVER. Yeah, we have a lot of that.
MISS GIRARD. Isn't that too bad! But they briefed us to expect a lot of that out here. (*Pause.*) Say, you haven't felt any yourself, have you?
PULVER. I guess I had a little touch of it . . . just a scratch.
MISS GIRARD. You know what you should do then? You should sleep more.
PULVER. Yeah.
MISS GIRARD. What's your job on the ship?
PULVER. Me? I'm . . . Executive Officer . . .
MISS GIRARD. But I thought that Executive Officers had to be at least a lieutenant . . .
PULVER. Say, you know what I was thinking? That we should have that little old drink of Scotcharoo right now ——
MISS GIRARD. I think so too. You know, I just love Scotch. I've just learned to drink it since I've joined the Army. But I'm already an absolute connoisseur.
PULVER. (*Dismayed.*) Oh, you are?
MISS GIRARD. My twin sister has a nickname for me that's partly because I like a particular brand of Scotch . . . (*Giggles.*) and partly because of a little personal characteristic about me that you

32

wouldn't understand. Do you know what she calls me? "Red Label!" (*They both laugh.*) What are you laughing at? You don't know what I'm talking about—and what's more you never will.

PULVER. What I was laughing about is—that's the kind I've got.

MISS GIRARD. Red Label! Perfect! But where can we drink it? This is a Navy ship . . . isn't it?

PULVER. Oh, yeah, yeah, we'll have to be careful . . . We mustn't be seen . . . Lemme see, where shall we go . . . (*Considers.*) I have it! We'll go back to my cabin. Nobody'd bother us there.

MISS GIRARD. Oh, you're what we nurses call a fast worker. But you look harmless to me.

PULVER. Oh, I don't know about that.

MISS GIRARD. What's your first name—Harmless?

PULVER. Frank.

MISS GIRARD. Hello, Frank. Mine's Ann.

PULVER. Hello, Ann.

MISS GIRARD. Where's the Scotch?

PULVER. Right this way. (*They start off toward* L. *passageway.* INSIGNA, MANNION, STEFANOWSKI, WILEY *and* LINDSTROM *enter from* R., *carrying the spy glass and binoculars.* STEFANOWSKI *trips on hatch cover.* MISS GIRARD *and* PULVER *turn.*) Hello, Mannion . . . Insigna . . . Stefanowski . . .

MANNION. (*Hoarsely.*) Hello, Mister Pulver . . .

PULVER. This is—Lieutenant Girard. (*The men murmur a greeting.*)

MISS GIRARD. What're you all doing with those glasses? (*More men crowd onto the stage.*)

PULVER. Well, don't work too hard . . . (*They turn to leave, but find themselves hemmed in by the men.*) It's getting a little stuffy up here, I guess we better . . . (ROBERTS *enters, very excited, carrying a piece of paper and a small book.*)

ROBERTS. (*Entering.*) Hey, Mannion . . . Everyone get a load of this . . . (*He stops short seeing* MISS GIRARD.)

PULVER. Hiya, Doug boy! This is Ann Girard—Doug Roberts.

ROBERTS. How do you do?

MISS GIRARD. (*Beaming.*) How do you do? You're Frank's roommate. He's told me all about you.

ROBERTS. Really?

MISS GIRARD. What are you doing on this ship?

33

ROBERTS. Now there you've got me.

MISS GIRARD. No, I mean what's your job? Like Frank here is Executive Officer.

ROBERTS. Oh, I'm just the Laundry and Morale Officer.

MISS GIRARD. Why, that's wonderful—I've just been made Laundry and Morale Officer for the nurses.

PULVER. I'm a dirty bastard! (MANNION *and* INSIGNA *begin an argument in whispers.*)

MISS GIRARD. We ought to get together and compare notes.

ROBERTS. I'd enjoy that very much.

PULVER. (*Attempting to usher* MISS GIRARD *off.*) Look, Doug. Will you excuse us? We're going down to have a little drink.

MISS GIRARD. Frank, aren't you going to ask Doug to join us?

PULVER. Hell, no—I mean—he doesn't like Scotch.

ROBERTS. That's right, Miss Girard. I stay true to alcohol and orange juice.

PULVER. Come on, Ann . . .

MISS GIRARD. Wait a minute! A lot of the girls swear by alcohol and orange juice. We ought to all have a party in our new dayroom.

INSIGNA. (*To* MANNION.) I bet you fifty bucks . . . (STEFANOWSKI *moves* INSIGNA *and* MANNION *away from* MISS GIRARD.)

MISS GIRARD. Seems to be an argument.

PULVER. Yeah. Some kinda discussion.

MISS GIRARD. Well, anyhow, we're fixing up a new dayroom. (*She looks offstage.*) Look, you can see it! Our new dormitory! That first window . . . (PULVER *takes glasses from* WILEY *to look at island.*)

INSIGNA. (*To* MANNION, *his voice rising.*) All right, I got a hundred bucks says that's the one with the birthmark on her ass. (*There is a terrible silence.* MISS GIRARD, *after a moment, takes the glasses from* PULVER *and looks at the island. After a moment she lowers the glasses and speaks to* PULVER.)

MISS GIRARD. Would you call the boat, please, Ensign Pulver? (*To* ROBERTS.) Good-bye, Doug. It was nice knowing you. You see, I promised the girls I'd help them hang some curtains in the window and I think we'd better get started, but immediately. Good-bye, everybody. (*To* MANNION.) Oh, what's your name again?

INSIGNA. Mine, sir?

34

MISS GIRARD. No. Yours.

MANNION. Mine? (MISS GIRARD *nods.*) Mannion.

MISS GIRARD. Well, Mannion, I'd advise you not to take that bet, because you'd lose a hundred bucks. (*To* PULVER.) Come on, Harmless. (*She exits, followed by a bewildered* PULVER. *The men watch her off.* STEFANOWSKI *throws his cap on the ground in anger.*)

MANNION. (*To* INSIGNA.) You loud-mouthed little bastard!

ROBERTS. Shut up! Insigna, how did you . . .

INSIGNA. We seen her taking a bath.

LINDSTROM. Through these glasses, Mister Roberts! They work perfect.

STEFANOWSKI. (*Furious.*) They can't see through curtains. (LINDSTROM *sighs. There is a little tragic moment.*)

ROBERTS. She's got a ten-minute boat ride. You've still got ten minutes.

WILEY. It wouldn't be any fun when you know you're going to be rushed.

LINDSTROM. This was the first real good day this bucket ever had.

ROBERTS. It still is. Listen. (*He reads from the paper in his hands.*) "On or about 1600 today, the AK 601 will proceed to Elysium Island, arriving there in seven days and reporting to the Port Director for cargo assignment." (*Emphatically.*) "During its stay in Elysium, the ship will make maximum use of the recreational facilities of this port." (*The men look up in slow surprise and disbelief.*)

STEFANOWSKI. But that means liberty!

ROBERTS. Yes.

INSIGNA. (*Dazed.*) Somebody must've been drunk to send us to a Liberty Port!

ROBERTS. Blind —— (*Now the men are excited.*)

WILEY. Elysium! Where's that?

MANNION. Yeah! Where's that, Mister Roberts? (*The men crowd around* ROBERTS *as he sits on the hatch.*)

ROBERTS. (*Reading from guide-book.*) "Elysium Island is often referred to as the 'Polynesian Paradise.' Vanilla, mother-of-pearl and rum are the chief exports."

INSIGNA. Did you hear that? Rum! (*He gooses* LINDSTROM.)

LINDSTROM. Cut that out! (DOLAN *gooses* INSIGNA.)

INSIGNA. Cut that out!

MANNION. Shut up!

ROBERTS. " Elysium City, its capital, is a beautiful metropolis of palm-lined boulevards, and colorful stucco homes. Since 1900, its population has remained remarkably constant at approximately 30,000."

INSIGNA. I'll fix that!

MANNION. (*The men shout him down.*) Go on, Mr. Roberts.

ROBERTS. That's all there is here, but there's one man on this ship who's been to Elysium.

STEFANOWSKI. Who's that?

MANNION. Who?

ROBERTS. Dowdy! (*The men run off wildly in every direction, shouting for* DOWDY. *The call is taken up all over the ship.* ROBERTS *listens to them happily, then notices a pair of binoculars. He looks toward the island for a moment, shrugs and is lifting the binoculars to his eyes as the lights*)

FADE OUT

SCENE 5

During the darkness we can hear the exciting strains of Polynesian music.

The lights come up slowly through a porthole, casting a strong late-afternoon shaft of light onto motionless white figures. It is the enlisted men's compartment below decks. Except for a few not yet fully dressed, the men are all in white uniforms. The compartment is a crowded place with three-tiered bunks against the bulkheads. Most of the men are crowded around the porthole, downstage L. The men who cannot see are listening to the reports of INSIGNA, *who is standing on a bench, looking out the porthole. The only man who is not galvanized with excitement is* DOWDY, *who sits calmly on a bench, downstage C., reading a magazine—" True Detective."*

GERHART. (*To* INSIGNA.) What do you see now, Sam?

INSIGNA. There's a lot of little boats up around the bow.

PAYNE. What kind of boats?

36

INSIGNA. Little sort of canoes and filled up with flowers, and women in them boats, paddling them . . .

PAYNE. Are they coming down this way?

INSIGNA. Naw.

STEFANOWSKI. Where's that music coming from?

INSIGNA. There's a great big canoe and it's all filled with fat bastards with flowers in their ears playing little old git-tars . . .

SCHLEMMER. Why the hell can't we go up on deck?

LINDSTROM. When the hell we going ashore! (INSIGNA *suddenly laughs.*)

PAYNE. What is it, Sam?

INSIGNA. I wish you could see this.

LINDSTROM. Lemme see, Sam.

INSIGNA. Some other time. (CHIEF JOHNSON *enters, looking knowingly at the men, shakes his head and addresses* DOWDY.)

JOHNSON. Same story in here, eh? Every porthole this side of the ship!

DOWDY. They're going to wear themselves down to a nub before they ever get over there. . . .

LINDSTROM. (*Takes coin from pocket and thrusts it at* INSIGNA.) Hey, Sam, here's another penny. Make them native kids down below dive for it.

INSIGNA. (*Impatiently.*) All right! (*Throws coin out the port.*) Heads up, you little bastards! (*The men watch tensely.*) Did he get it? Yep. Hey, Dowdy—where's that little park again? Where you said all the good-looking women hang out?

DOWDY. For the last time—you see that big hill over there to the right . . .

INSIGNA. Yeah.

DOWDY. You see a big church . . .

INSIGNA. Yeah.

DOWDY. Pass that church.

INSIGNA. Yeah, I'm past it.

DOWDY. That's the park.

INSIGNA. Well, I'll be damned . . .

LINDSTROM. Hey, show me that park, Sam? (*The other men gather around* INSIGNA, *asking to see the park.*)

INSIGNA. (*The authority now.*) All right, you bastards, line up. I'll show you where the women hang out. (*The men form a line and each steps up to the porthole where* INSIGNA *points out the park.)*

JOHNSON. *(To* DOWDY.*)* Hey, Dowdy, smell that shoe polish? These guys have gone nuts!

DOWDY. I went down the ship's store the other day to buy a bar of soap and, do you know, they been sold out for a week! No soap, no Listerine, no Mum! Nothin'! *(*DOLAN, *wearing the messenger's belt, enters. The men greet him excitedly.)*

STEFANOWSKI. What's the word on liberty, Dolan?

DOLAN. The old man's still asleep.

INSIGNA. I'll get him up! I'm going up there and tap on his door! *(Picks up a heavy lead pipe.)*

DOWDY. *(Grabbing* INSIGNA.*)* Like hell you are! You're going to stay right here and pray. You're going to pray that he wakes up feeling good and decides he's kept you guys sweating long enough!

MANNION. That's telling the little crud! *(*INSIGNA *and* MANNION *threaten each other.* DOLAN *is interrupted by the sound of static on the squawk box. Instantly all men turn toward it eagerly.)*

DOLAN. *(On squawk box.)* Now hear this! Now hear this!

WILEY. Here we go! Here we go!

STEFANOWSKI. *(Imitating the squawk box.)* Liberty . . . will commence . . . immediately!

GERHART. Quiet!

DOLAN. *(On squawk box.)* Now hear this! The Captain's messenger will report to the Captain's cabin on the double!

DOLAN. He's awake! *(He runs out.)*

PAYNE. Won't be long now!

MANNION. Get into those whites! We're going to be the first ones over the side! Give me a hand! *(Now there is a general frenzy of preparation—the men put the last-minute touches to shoes, hair, uniforms.)*

GERHART. *(Singing to the tune of " California, Here I Come.")*
        Ee-liss-ee-um, here I come! . . .
        Ta-ta-ta-ta-ta-da-tah . . .

SCHLEMMER. *(To* GERHART.*)* Watch where you're going! I just polished that shoe.

INSIGNA. *(These men gather around him.* LINDSTROM *remains unhappily alone.)* Now listen, you guys! Stefanowski and me are going to work alone for the first hour and a half! But if you pick up something first . . . *(Produces small map from his pocket.)*

We'll be working up and down this street here . . . (*They study the map. Now the squawk box is clicked on again. All the men stand rigid, listening.*)

DOLAN. (*On squawk box.*) Now hear this! The Captain is now going to make a personal announcement. (*Sound of squawk-box switch.*)

CAPTAIN. (*On squawk box.*) How the hell does this thing work? (*Sound of squawk-box switch again.*) This is the Captain speaking. I just woke up from a little nap and I got a surprise. I found out there were men on this ship who were expecting liberty. (*At this point, the lights start dimming until the entire scene is blacked out. The speech continues throughout the darkness. Under the CAPTAIN's speech the strains of Polynesian music can be heard.*) Now I don't know how such a rumor got around, but I'd like to clear it up right now. You see, it's like this. Because of cargo requirements and security conditions which has just come to my personal attention there will be no liberty as long as we're in this here port. And one other thing—as long as we're here, no man will wear white uniforms. Now I would like to repeat for the benefit of complete understanding and clearness, NO LIBERTY. That is all.

SCENE 6

The lights come up on the CAPTAIN's cabin. Against the L. bulkhead is a settee. A chair is placed C. Up C. is the only door. The CAPTAIN is seated behind his desk, holding a watch in one hand and the microphone in the other, in an attitude of waiting. Just over the desk and against the R. bulkhead is a ship's intercommunication board. There is a wall-safe in the R. bulkhead. After a moment there is a knock on the door.

CAPTAIN. Come in, Mister Roberts. (*As ROBERTS enters, the CAPTAIN puts the microphone on the desk.*) I been expectin' you.

ROBERTS. Okay, what about it—when does this crew get liberty?

CAPTAIN. Well, in the first place, just kinda hold your tongue.

ROBERTS. When are you going to let this crew go ashore?

CAPTAIN. I'm not. This wasn't my idea—coming to a Liberty Port. One of my officers arranged it with a certain Port Director—gave him a bottle of Scotch whiskey—compliments of the Captain.

The Port Director was kind enough to send me a little thank-you note along with our orders. Sit down, Mister Roberts. (ROBERTS *sits.*) I'll admit I was a little pre-voked about not being consulted. Then I got to thinking maybe we oughta come to this port anyway so's you and me could have a little talk.

ROBERTS. Let's quit wasting time. Don't you hear that music? Don't you know it's tearing those guys apart?

CAPTAIN. (*Rises, goes to* ROBERTS.) Now you listen to me. I got two things I want to show you. (*He unlocks the wall-safe, opens it and takes out a commander's cap with gold braid " scrambled eggs" on the visor.*) That's the cap of a full commander. I'm gonna wear that cap some day and you're going to help me. (*Replaces cap in safe, goes back to* ROBERTS.) I guess there's no harm in telling you that you helped me get that palm tree by working cargo. Now don't let this go to your head, but when Admiral Finchley awarded me that palm tree, he said, "You got a good Cargo Officer, Morton; keep him at it, you're going places." So I went out and bought that hat. There's nothing gonna stand between me and that hat—certainly not you. Now last week I told you there wasn't going to be any more letters. But what do I find on my desk this morning . . . (*Taking letter from desk.*) Another letter that says " friction between myself and the Commanding Officer." That ain't gonna go in, Mister.

ROBERTS. How are you going to stop it, Captain?

CAPTAIN. I ain't, you are. (*Goes to his chair and sits.*) Just how much do you want this crew to have a liberty anyhow? Enough to stop this " friction "? (*Leans forward.*) Enough to stop writing letters ever? Because that's the only way this crew is gonna get ashore today—or any other day. (*Leans back.*) Well, we've had our little talk. What do you say?

ROBERTS. (*After a moment.*) How did you get in the Navy? How did you get on our side? You're what I joined to fight *against.* You ignorant, arrogant, ambitious . . . (*Rises.*) jackass! Keeping a hundred and sixty-seven men in prison because you got a palm tree for the work *they* did. I don't know which I hate worse—you or that other malignant growth that stands outside your door!

CAPTAIN. Why, you stinking little ——

ROBERTS. How did you ever get command of a ship? I realize that in wartime they have to scrape the bottom of the barrel, but where the hell did they ever scrape you up?

CAPTAIN. (*Shouting.*) There's just one thing left for you—a general court-martial.

ROBERTS. That suits me fine. Court-martial me!

CAPTAIN. You've got it!

ROBERTS. I'm asking for it!

CAPTAIN. You don't have to ask for it, you've got it now!

ROBERTS. If I can't get transferred off here, I'll get court-martialed off! I'm fed up! But you'll need a witness. Send for your messenger. He's down below. I'll say it all again in front of him. (*Pauses.*) Go on, call in Dolan! (*The* CAPTAIN *doesn't move.*) Go on, call him. (*Still the* CAPTAIN *doesn't move.*) Do you want me to call him?

CAPTAIN. No. (*He walks upstage, then turns to* ROBERTS.) I think you're a pretty smart boy. I may not talk very good, Mister, but I know now to take care of smart boys. Let me tell you a little secret. I hate your guts, you college son-of-a-bitch! You think you're better than I am! You think you're better because you've had everything handed to you! Let me tell you something, Mister —I've worked since I was ten years old, and all my life I've known you superior bastards. I knew you people when I was a kid in Boston and I worked in eating-places and you ordered me around. . . . "Oh, bus-boy! My friend here seems to have thrown up on the table. Clean it up, please." I started going to sea as a steward and I worked for you then . . . "Steward, take my magazine out to the deck chair!" . . . "Steward, I don't like your looks. Please keep out of my way as much as possible!" Well, I took that crap! I took that for years from pimple-faced bastards who weren't good enough to wipe my nose! And now I don't have to take it any more! There's a war on, and I'm the Captain, Mister, I'm the Captain, and you're welcome to wipe my nose! The worst thing I can do to you is to keep you on this ship! And that's where you're going to stay! Now get out of here! (*He goes to his chair and sits.* ROBERTS *moves slowly toward the door. He hears the music, goes to the porthole and listens. Then he turns to the* CAPTAIN.)

ROBERTS. Can't you hear that music, Captain?

CAPTAIN. Yeah, I hear it. (*Busies himself at desk, ignoring* ROBERTS.)

ROBERTS. Don't you know those guys below can hear it too? Oh, my God.

CAPTAIN. Get out of here. (*After a moment,* ROBERTS *turns from the porthole and slumps against the* CAPTAIN'S *locker. His face is strained.*)

ROBERTS. What do you want for liberty, Captain?

CAPTAIN. I want plenty. You're through writin' letters—ever.

ROBERTS. Okay.

CAPTAIN. That's not all. You're through givin' me trouble. You're through talkin' back to me in front of the crew. You ain't even gonna open your mouth—except in civil answer. (ROBERTS *doesn't answer.*) Mister Roberts, you know that if you don't take my terms I'll let you go out that door and that's the end of any hope for liberty.

ROBERTS. Is that all, Captain?

CAPTAIN. No. Anyone know you're in here?

ROBERTS. No one.

CAPTAIN. Then you won't go blabbin' about this to anyone ever. It might not sound so good. And besides I don't want you to take credit for gettin' this crew ashore.

ROBERTS. Do you think I'm doing this for credit? Do you think I'd *let* anyone know about this?

CAPTAIN. I gotta be sure.

ROBERTS. You've got my word, that's all.

CAPTAIN. (*After a pause.*) Your word. Yes, you college fellas make a big show about keeping your word.

ROBERTS. How about it, Captain. Is it a deal?

CAPTAIN. Yeah. (ROBERTS *picks up the microphone, turns on a switch and thrusts the microphone at the* CAPTAIN.) Now hear this. This is the Captain speaking. I've got some further word on security conditions in this port and so it gives me great pleasure to tell you that liberty, for the starboard section . . .

ROBERTS. (*Covering the microphone with his hand.*) For the entire crew, every single one of them.

CAPTAIN. Correction: Liberty for the entire crew will commence immediately. (ROBERTS *turns off the microphone. After a moment we hear the shouts of the crew.* ROBERTS *goes up to porthole. The* CAPTAIN *leans back on his chair. A song, "Roll Me Over," is started by someone and is soon taken up by the whole crew.*)

ROBERTS. (*Looking out of the porthole. He is excited and happy.*) Listen to those crazy bastards. Listen to them. (*The crew con-*

tinues to sing with increasing volume. Now the words can be dis-
tinguished:

> Roll me over in the clover,
> Roll me over, lay me down
> And do it again.)

THE CURTAIN FALLS

ACT II

Scene 1

(*Before curtain rises sound of winch starts on cue [record], also following offstage:*)

VOICE. Okay, Lieutenant, we're loaded! Start the winch! (*Sound of winch.*)

ROBERTS. Okay, start the winch! Hey ——

VOICE. Schlemmer, look out!

ROBERTS. Let her in easy!

VOICE. Let her in easy! (*Curtain rises. Three seamen on hatch cover may be in makeshift cargo net, which may be held taut on a line from flies, and slacked off as soon as curtain rises.*)

> *The curtain rises on the main set. It is now 3:45 A. M. The night is pitch-black, but we can see because of a light over the head of the gangway, where a temporary desk has been rigged, a large ship's logbook lies open on this desk. A small table on which are hospital supplies is at L. of the door.*
>
> *At rise, ROBERTS, DOC, LINDSTROM, JOHNSON, DOWDY and four SEAMEN are discovered onstage. LINDSTROM, in web belt, is writing in the log. ROBERTS is standing with a pile of yellow slips in his hand, he wears the side-arms of the Officer of the Deck. JOHNSON and a SEAMAN are standing near the hatchway, holding the inert body of another SEAMAN, who has court plaster on his face. Three SEAMEN lie on the hatch cover where DOC is kneeling, bandaging one of them. As the curtain rises we hear the sound of a siren off R. Everyone turns and looks —that is, everyone who is conscious. After net slack off.*

ROBERTS. Well, they're peaceful, anyhow.

LINDSTROM. Here's another batch, Mister Roberts—a whole paddy wagon full.

JOHNSON. (*To DOC, indicating body he is carrying.*) Where do we put number twenty-three here, Doc? Sick bay or what?

44

DOC. Just put him to bed. His condition's only critical.

JOHNSON. (*Carrying* SEAMAN *off.*) Now I'm stacking 'em on the deck down there—I'm on the third layer already. (JOHNSON *and* DOWDY *carry men off down hatch.*)

LINDSTROM. We got the record now, Mister Roberts! This makes the seventh batch since we went on watch! (*At this point a* SHORE PATROLMAN *enters from the gangway.*)

SHORE PATROLMAN. (*Handing* ROBERTS *a sheaf of yellow slips.*) For your collection. (*Points down gangway.*) Take a look at them.

ROBERTS. (*Looks offstage.*) My God, what did they do?

SHORE PATROLMAN. They done all right, Lieutenant. Five of them busted into a formal dance and took on a hundred and twenty-eight Army bastards. (*Calls off.*) All right, let's go! (STEFANOW-SKI, GERHART, PAYNE *and* MANNION, *with his arm around* INSIGNA, *straggle on—a frightening sight—followed by a* MILITARY POLICE-MAN. INSIGNA'S *uniform is torn to shreds.* MANNION *is clad in a little diaper of crepe paper. All have bloody faces and uniforms. A few bear souvenirs—a Japanese lantern, leis, Army caps, a Shore Patrol band, etc. They throw perfunctory salutes to the colors, then murmur a greeting to* ROBERTS.)

MILITARY POLICEMAN. Duty Officer?

ROBERTS. That's right.

MILITARY POLICEMAN. (*Salutes.*) Colonel Middleton presents his compliments to the Captain and wishes him to know that these men made a shambles out of the Colonel's testimonial dinner-dance.

ROBERTS. Is this true, Insigna?

INSIGNA. That's right, Mister Roberts. A shambles. (*To* MANNION.) Ain't that right, Killer?

MANNION. That's right, Mister Roberts.

ROBERTS. You men crashed a dance for Army personnel?

MANNION. Yes, sir! And they made us feel unwelcome!

ROBERTS. Oh, the Army started a fight, eh?

GERHART. No, sir! *We* started it!

STEFANOWSKI. We finished it too! (*To* MILITARY POLICEMAN.) Tell Mister Roberts how many of you Army bastards are in the hospital.

MANNION. Go on.

MILITARY POLICEMAN. Thirty-eight soldiers of the United States

Army have been hospitalized. And the Colonel himself has a very bad bruise on his left shin! (PAYNE *merely points to himself*.) And that isn't all, Lieutenant. There were young ladies present— fifty of them. Colonel Middleton had been lining them up for a month, from the finest families of Elysium. And he had personally guaranteed their safety this evening. Well, sir . . .

ROBERTS. Well?

MILITARY POLICEMAN. Two of those young ladies got somewhat mauled, one actually got a black eye, six of them got their clothes torn off and then went screaming off into the night and they haven't been heard from since. What are you going to do about it, Lieutenant?

ROBERTS. Well, I'm due to get relieved here in fifteen minutes— I'll be glad to lead a search party.

MILITARY POLICEMAN. No, sir. The Army's taking care of that end. The Colonel will want to know what punishment you're going to give these men.

ROBERTS. Tell the Colonel that I'm sure our Captain will think of something.

MILITARY POLICEMAN. But . . .

ROBERTS. That's all, Sergeant.

MILITARY POLICEMAN. (*Salutes*.) Thank you, sir. (*He goes off*.)

SHORE PATROLMAN. Lieutenant, I been pretty sore at your guys up till now—we had to put on ten extra Shore Patrolmen on account of this ship. But if you knew Colonel " Chicken " Middleton— well, I'd be willing to do this every night. (*To the men*.) So long, fellows! (*The men call " So long." SHORE PATROLMAN exits, saluting ROBERTS and quarter-deck*.)

ROBERTS. Well, what've you got to say for yourselves?

STEFANOWSKI. (*After a moment*.) Okay if we go ashore again, Mister Roberts?

ROBERTS. (*To LINDSTROM*.) Is this the first time for these guys?

LINDSTROM. (*Showing log*.) Yes, sir, they got a clean record— they only been brought back once.

ROBERTS. What do you say, Doc? (*The men turn eagerly to DOC*.)

DOC. Anybody got a fractured skull?

MEN. No.

DOC. Okay, you pass the physical.

ROBERTS. Go down and take a shower first and get into some clothes. (*The men rush to the hatchway*.)

46

STEFANOWSKI. We still got time to get back to that dance! (*As they descend hatchway,* INSIGNA *pulls crepe paper from around* MANNION *as he is halfway down the hatchway.*)

ROBERTS. How you feeling, Doc?

DOC. These alcohol fumes are giving me a cheap drunk—otherwise pretty routine. (*Takes box from table and gestures for men to remove table. They carry it off.*)

ROBERTS. What have you got in the box?

DOC. (*Descending hatchway—holding up small packet he has taken from the box.*) Little favors from the Doc. (*His head disappears.*)

LINDSTROM. I wish Wiley would get back here and relieve me. I've got to get over to that island before it runs out of women. (DOLAN *enters from gangway.*)

DOLAN. Howdy, Mister Roberts! I'm drunk as a goat! (*Pulls a goat aboard.*) Show him how drunk I am. Mister Roberts, when I first saw her she was eatin', and you know, she just eat her way into my heart. She was eatin' a little old palm tree and I thought to myself, our ship needs a mascot. (*He points out palm tree to goat.*) There you are, kid. Chow! (ROBERTS *blocks his way.*)

ROBERTS. Wait a minute . . . wait a minute. What's her name?

DOLAN. I don't know, sir.

ROBERTS. She's got a name plate.

DOLAN. Oh, so she has . . . her name is . . . (*Reads from tag on goat's collar.*) Property Of.

ROBERTS. What's her last name?

DOLAN. Her last name . . . (*Reads again.*) Rear Admiral Wentworth. (*Approaching siren is heard offstage.*)

ROBERTS. Okay, Dolan, hit the sack. I'll take care of her.

DOLAN. Okay, Mister Roberts. (*Descends hatchway.*) See that she gets a good square meal. (*He points to the* CAPTAIN'S *palm tree and winks, then disappears.* GERHART *enters from gangway.*)

LINDSTROM. Hey, Wiley, where have you been? (LINDSTROM *frantically removes his web belt and shoves it at* WILEY.)

WILEY. Okay, okay—you're relieved.

LINDSTROM. (*Tosses a fast salute to* ROBERTS *and says in one breath.*) Requestpermissiontogoashore! (*He hurries down gangway.* SHORE PATROLMAN *enters from gangway.*)

SHORE PATROLMAN. Lieutenant, has one of your men turned up with a . . . (*Sees goat and takes leash.*) Oh, thanks. (*To goat.*)

Come on, come on, your papa over there is worried about you. (*Pulls goat down gangway.*)

WILEY. Where's your relief, Mister Roberts?

ROBERTS. (*Sitting on hatch.*) He'll be along any minute. How was your liberty, Wiley? (WILEY *grins. So does* ROBERTS. DOC *enters from hatchway.*)

DOC. What are you looking so cocky about anyway?

ROBERTS. Am I looking cocky? Maybe it's because for the first time since I've been on this ship, I'm seeing a crew.

DOC. What do you think you've been living with all this time?

ROBERTS. Just a hundred and sixty-seven separate guys. There's a big difference, Doc. Now these guys are bound together. You saw Insigna and Mannion. Doc, I think these guys are strong enough now to take all the miserable, endless days ahead of us. I only hope I'm strong enough.

DOC. Doug, tomorrow you and I are going over there and take advantage of the groundwork that's been laid tonight. You and I are going to have ourselves a liberty. (PULVER *enters slowly from the gangway and walks across the stage.* DOC *calls* ROBERTS' *attention to him.*)

ROBERTS. Hello, Frank. How was your liberty? (PULVER *half turns.*)

PULVER. Broke my record. (SHORE PATROL OFFICER *enters from gangway, and calls offstage. He speaks with a Southern accent.*)

SHORE PATROL OFFICER. That's your post and that's your post. You know what to do. (*He salutes the quarter-deck, then* ROBERTS.) Officer of the Deck? (ROBERTS *nods. The* SHORE PATROL OFFICER *hesitates a moment.*) I hope you don't mind but I've stationed two of my men at the foot of the gangway. I'm sorry but this ship is restricted for the rest of its stay in Elysium. Your Captain is to report to the Island Commander at seven o'clock this morning. I'd recommend that he's there on time. The Admiral's a pretty tough cookie when he's mad, and he's madder now than I've ever seen him.

ROBERTS. What in particular did this?

SHORE PATROL LIEUTENANT. A little while ago six men from your ship broke into the home of the French Consul and started throwing things through the plate-glass living-room window. We found some of the things on the lawn: a large world globe, a small love seat, a lot of books and a bust of Balzac—the French writer. We also found an Army private first class who was unconscious at the time. He claims they threw him too.

ROBERTS. Through the window?

SHORE PATROL LIEUTENANT. That's right! It seems he took them there for a little joke. He didn't tell them it was the Consul's house; he said it was a—what we call in Alabama—a cat-house. (ROBERTS *and* DOC *nod.*) Be sure that your Captain is there at seven o'clock sharp. If it makes you feel any better, Admiral Wentworth says this is the worst ship he's ever seen in his entire naval career. (*Laughs, then salutes.*) Good night, Lieutenant.

ROBERTS. (*Returning salute.*) Good night. (*The* SHORE PATROL LIEUTENANT *exits down gangway—saluting the quarter-deck.*)

WILEY. Well, there goes the liberty. That was sure a wham-bam-thank you, ma'am!

DOC. Good night. (*He exits through* L. *passageway.*)

WILEY. But, by God, it was worth it. That liberty was worth anything!

ROBERTS. I think you're right, Wiley.

WILEY. Hunh?

ROBERTS. I think you're right.

WILEY. Yeah. (*He smiles.* ROBERTS *looks over the log.* WILEY *whistles softly to himself " Roll Me Over " as the lights slowly*)

FADE OUT

(*During the darkness we hear* JOHNSON *shouting:*)

JOHNSON. All right, fall in for muster. Form two ranks. And pipe down.

SCENE 2

The lights come up, revealing the deck. Morning sunlight. A group of men, R. *and* L., *in orderly formation. They are talking.*

JOHNSON. 'Ten-shun! (*The command is relayed through the ship. The* CAPTAIN *enters from his cabin, followed by* ROBERTS. *The* CAPTAIN *steps up on the hatch cover.* ROBERTS *starts to fall in with the men.*)

CAPTAIN. (*Calling to* ROBERTS *and pointing to a place beside him-*

49

self on hatch cover.) Over here, Roberts. (ROBERTS *takes his place* L. *of* CAPTAIN.) We're being kicked out of this port. I had a feeling this liberty was a bad idea. That's why we'll never have one again. We're going to erase this blot from my record if we have to work twenty-four hours a day. We're going to move even more cargo than we've ever moved before. And if there ain't enough cargo work, Mister Roberts here is gonna find some. Isn't that right, Mister Roberts? (ROBERTS *doesn't answer.*) Isn't that right, Mister Roberts?

ROBERTS. Yes, sir.

CAPTAIN. I'm appointing Mister Roberts here and now to see that you men toe the line. And I can't think of a more honorable man for the job. He's a man who keeps his word no matter what. (*Turns to* ROBERTS.) Now, Roberts, if you do a good job—and if the Admiral begins to smile on us again—there might be something in it for you. What would you say if that little silver bar on your collar got a twin brother some day? (ROBERTS *is startled. The* CAPTAIN *calls offstage.*) Officer of the Deck!

OFFSTAGE VOICE. Yes, sir!

CAPTAIN. (*To* ROBERTS.) You wasn't expectin' that, was you? (*Calling offstage.*) Get ready to sail!

OFFSTAGE VOICE. Aye-aye, sir!

CAPTAIN. You men are dismissed!

JOHNSON. Fall out! (*The men fall out. Some exit. A little group forms downstage.*)

CAPTAIN. Wait a minute! Wait a minute! Roberts, take these men here back aft to handle lines. And see that they work up a sweat. (ROBERTS *and men look at him.*) Did you hear me, Roberts? I gave you an order!

ROBERTS. (*Carefully.*) Yes, Captain. I heard you.

CAPTAIN. How do you answer when I give an order?

ROBERTS. (*After a pause.*) Aye-aye, sir.

CAPTAIN. That's more like it . . . that's more like it! (*He exits into his cabin.*)

STEFANOWSKI. What'd he mean, Mister Roberts?

ROBERTS. I don't know. Just what he said, I guess.

GERHART. What'd you let him give you all that guff for?

DOLAN. (*Stepping up on hatch, carrying a file folder.*) Because he's tired, that's why. He had the mid-watch last night. Your tail'd be dragging too if you had to handle all them customers.

ROBERTS. Come on. Let's get going . . .

DOLAN. Wait a minute, Mister Roberts. Something come for you in the mail this morning—a little love letter from the Bureau. (*Pulls out paper from file folder.*) Get a load of this! (*Reads.*) "To All Ships and Stations: Heightened war offensive has created urgent need aboard combat ships for experienced officers. (*He clicks his teeth and winks at* ROBERTS.) All commanding officers are hereby directed to forward with their endorsements all applications for transfer from officers with twenty-four months' sea duty." (ROBERTS *grabs the directive and reads it.* DOLAN *looks at* ROBERTS *and smiles.*) You got twenty-nine months—you're the only officer aboard that has. Mister Roberts, the Old Man is hanging on the ropes from the working-over the Admiral give him. All he needs to flatten him is one more little jab. And here it is. Your letter. I typed it up. (*He pulls out triplicate letter from file cover—then a fountain pen which he offers to* ROBERTS.) Sign it and I'll take it in ——

MANNION. Go on, sign it, Mister Roberts. He'll take off like a bird.

DOLAN. What're you waitin' for, Mister Roberts?

ROBERTS. (*Handing directive back to* DOLAN.) I'll want to look it over first, Dolan. Come on, let's get going.

DOLAN. There's nothing to look over. This is the same letter we wrote yesterday—only quoting this new directive.

ROBERTS. Look, Dolan, I'm tired. And I told you I wanted ——

DOLAN. You ain't too tired to sign your name!

ROBERTS. (*Sharply.*) Take it easy, Dolan. I'm not going to sign it. So take it easy! (*Turns to exit* R., *finds himself blocked by crew.*) Did you hear me? Let's get going! (*Exits.*)

STEFANOWSKI. What the hell's come over him? (*They look at one another.*)

INSIGNA. Aye-aye, sir—for cripes' sake!

MANNION. (*After a moment.*) Come on. Let's get going.

DOLAN. (*Bitterly.*) "Take it easy . . . take it easy!" (*The men start to move off slowly as the lights*)

FADE OUT

(*During the darkness we hear a radio. There is considerable static.*)

AMERICAN BROADCASTER. Still, of course, we have no official word from the Headquarters of the Supreme Allied Command in Europe. I repeat, there is no official announcement yet. The report that the war in Europe has ended has come from only one correspondent. It has not been confirmed by other correspondents or by SHAEF headquarters. But here is one highly intriguing fact— that report has not been denied either in Washington or in SHAEF headquarters in Europe. IT HAS NOT BEEN DENIED. Right now in those places the newsmen are crowded, waiting to flash to the world the announcement of V-E Day.

SCENE 3

The lights come up on ROBERTS' *and* PULVER'S *cabin.* DOC, *at the desk, and* PULVER, *up in his bunk, are listening to the radio.*

PULVER. Turn that damn thing off, Doc. Has Doug ever said anything to you about wanting a promotion?

DOC. Of course not. I doubt if he's even conscious of what rank he is.

PULVER. You can say that again!

DOC. I doubt if he's even conscious of what rank he is.

PULVER. That's what I said. He doesn't even think about a promotion. The only thing he thinks about is the war news—up in the radio shack two weeks now—all day long—listening with a headset, reading all the bulletins. . . . Anyone who says he's bucking for another stripe is a dirty liar.

DOC. Who says he is, Frank?

PULVER. Insigna, Mannion and some of the other guys. I heard them talking outside the porthole. They were talking loud on purpose so I could hear them—they must've guessed I was lying here on my bunk. What's happened to Doug anyway, Doc?

DOC. How would I know! He's spoken about ten words to me in as many days. But I'm damn well going to find out.

PULVER. He won't talk, Doc. This morning I followed him all around the room while he was shaving. I begged him to talk to me. I says, "You're a fellow who needs a friend and here I am." And I says, "What's all this trouble you're having with the crew? You tell me and I'll fix it up like that." And then I give him some real good advice—I says, "Keep your chin up," and things like

52

that. And then do you know what he did? He walked out of the room just as if I wasn't here, and I was here. (*There is a knock on the door.*)

DOC. Come in. (DOWDY *enters.*)

DOWDY. Doc, Mister Pulver—could we see you officers a minute?

DOC. Sure. (GERHART *and* LINDSTROM *enter, closing the door.*) What is it?

DOWDY. Tell them what happened, Gerhart.

GERHART. Well, sir, I sure don't like to say this but . . . Mister Roberts just put Dolan on report.

LINDSTROM. Me and Gerhart seen him.

PULVER. On report!

GERHART. Yes, sir. Tomorrow morning Dolan has to go up before the Captain—on account of Mister Roberts.

LINDSTROM. On account of Mister Roberts.

GERHART. And we was wondering if you officers could get him to take Dolan off report before . . . well, before ——

DOC. Before what, Gerhart?

GERHART. Well, you see, the guys are all down in the compartment, talking about it. And they're saying some pretty rough things about Mister Roberts. Nobody just ever expected to see him put a man on report and . . .

LINDSTROM. He ain't gonna turn out to be like an officer, is he, Doc?

DOWDY. Lindstrom . . .

LINDSTROM. Oh, I didn't mean you, Doc . . . or even you, Mister Pulver!

DOC. That's all right, Lindstrom. What was this trouble with Dolan?

DOWDY. This letter business again!

GERHART. Yes, sir. Dolan was just kiddin' him about not sending in any more letters. And all of a sudden Mister Roberts turned just white and yelled, "Shut up, Dolan. Shut your damn mouth. I've had enough." And Dolan naturally got snotty back at him and Mister Roberts put him right on report.

LINDSTROM. Right on report. (ROBERTS *enters.*)

PULVER. Hello, Doug boy. Aren't you listening to the war news?

DOWDY. Okay, Doc. We'll get that medical store room cleaned out tomorrow. (DOWDY, GERHART *and* LINDSTROM *leave.*)

PULVER. We thought you were up in the radio shack.

ROBERTS. (*To* PULVER.) Don't you want to go down to the wardroom and have a cup of coffee?

PULVER. (*Jumping down from bunk.*) Sure. I'll go with you.

ROBERTS. I don't want any. Why don't you go ahead?

PULVER. Nah. (*He sits back on bunk. There is another little pause.*)

ROBERTS. Will you go on out anyway? I want to talk to Doc.

PULVER. (*Rising and crossing to door.*) All right, I will. I'm going for a cup of coffee. (*Stops, turns and gets cap from top of locker.*) No, I'm not! I'm going up to the radio shack. You aren't the only one interested in the war news. See you later, Doc. (*He exits.*)

ROBERTS. (*With emotion.*) Doc, transfer me, will you? (DOC *looks at him.*) Transfer me to the hospital on this next island! You can do it. You don't need the Captain's approval! Just put me ashore for examination—say there's something wrong with my eyes or my feet or my head! You can trump up something!

DOC. What good would that do?

ROBERTS. Plenty! I could lie around that hospital for a couple of weeks. The ship would have sailed—I'd have missed it! I'd be off this ship. Will you do it, Doc?

DOC. Doug, why did you put Dolan on report just now?

ROBERTS. (*Angrily.*) I gave him an order and he didn't carry it out fast enough to suit me. (*Glares at* DOC, *who just studies him.* ROBERTS *rises and paces* R.) No, that's not true. It was the war. I just heard the news. The war was ending and I couldn't get to it and there was Dolan giving me guff about something—and all of a sudden I hated him. I hated all of them. I was sick of the sullen bastards staring at me as though I'd sold them down the river or something. If they think I'm bucking for a promotion—if they're stupid enough to think I'd walk ten feet across the room to get anything from that Captain, then I'm through with the whole damn ungrateful mob!

DOC. Does this crew owe you something?

ROBERTS. What the hell do you mean by that?

DOC. You talk as if they did. (ROBERTS *rises and crosses to bunk.*)

ROBERTS. (*Quietly.*) That's exactly how I'm talking. I didn't realize it but that's exactly the way I've been feeling. That shows you how far gone I am, Doc. I've been taking something out on them. I've been blaming them for something that . . .

54

DOC. What, Doug? Something what? You've made some sort of an agreement with the Captain, haven't you, Doug!

ROBERTS. (*Turns.*) Agreement? I don't know what you mean. Will you transfer me, Doc?

DOC. Not a chance, Doug. I could never get away with it—you know that.

PULVER. (*Offstage.*) Doug! Doc! (*Entering.*) Listen to the radio, you uninformed bastards! Turn it up! (ROBERTS *reaches over and turns up the radio. The excited voice of an announcer can be heard.*)

ANNOUNCER. . . . this broadcast to bring you a special news flash! The war is over in Europe! THE WAR IS OVER IN EUROPE! (ROBERTS *grasps* DOC'S *arm in excitement.*) Germany has surrendered unconditionally to the Allied Armies. The surrender was signed in a schoolhouse in the city of Rheims . . . (ROBERTS *stands staring.* DOC *turns off the radio. For a moment there is silence, then:*)

DOC. I would remind you that there's still a minor skirmish here in the Pacific.

ROBERTS. I'll miss that one too. But to hell with me. This is the greatest day in the world. We're going to celebrate. How about it, Frank?

PULVER. Yeah, Doug. We've got to celebrate!

DOC. (*Starting to pull alcohol from waste basket.*) What'll it be— alcohol and orange juice or orange juice and alcohol?

ROBERTS. No, that's not good enough.

PULVER. Hell, no, Doc! (*He looks expectantly at* ROBERTS.)

ROBERTS. We've got to think of something that'll lift this ship right out of the water and turn it around the other way. (PULVER *suddenly rises to his feet.*)

PULVER. (*Shouting.*) Doug! Oh, why didn't I think of this before? Doug! Doc! You're going to blow your tops when you hear the idea I got! What a smart little bastard of an idea! It's the only thing to do. It's the only thing in the whole world to do! That's all! Doug, you said I never had any ideas. You said I never finished anything I started. Well, you're wrong—tonight you're wrong! I thought of something and I finished it. I was going to save it for your birthday, but I'm going to give it to you tonight, because we gotta celebrate . . .

ROBERTS. (*Waves his hands in* PULVER'S *face for attention.*) Wait a minute, Frank! What is it?

PULVER. A firecracker, dammit! (*He reaches under his mattress and pulls out a large, wobbly firecracker which has been painted red.*) We're gonna throw a firecracker under the Old Man's bunk. Bam-bam-bam! Wake up, you old son-of-a-bitch, IT'S V-E DAY!

ROBERTS. (*Rising.*) Frank!

PULVER. Look at her, Doc. Ain't it a beauty? Ain't that the greatest hand-made, hand-painted, hand-packed firecracker you ever saw?

ROBERTS. (*Smiling and taking firecracker.*) Yes, Frank. That's the most beautiful firecracker I ever saw in my life. But will it work?

PULVER. Sure it'll work. At least, I think so.

ROBERTS. Haven't you tested it? It's got to work, Frank, it's just got to work!

PULVER. I'll tell you what I'll do. I'll take it down to the laundry and test it—that's my laboratory, the laundry. I got all the fixings down there—powder, fuses, everything, all hid behind the soap-flakes. And if this one works, I can make another one in two minutes.

ROBERTS. Okay, Frank. Take off. We'll wait for you here. (PULVER *starts off.*) Be sure you got enough to make it loud. What'd you use for powder?

PULVER. Loud! This ain't a popgun. This is a firecracker. I used fulminate of mercury. I'll be right back. (*He runs out.*)

ROBERTS. Fulminate of mercury! That stuff's murder! Do you think he means it?

DOC. (*Taking alcohol bottle from waste basket.*) Of course not. Where could he get fulminate of mercury?

ROBERTS. I don't know. He's pretty resourceful.

DOC. How about a drink, Doug? (*He pours alcohol and orange juice into two glasses.*)

ROBERTS. Right! Doc, I been living with a genius. This makes it all worth while—the whole year and a half he spent in his bunk. How else could you celebrate V-E Day? A firecracker under the Old Man's bunk! The silly little son-of-a-bitch!

DOC. (*Handing* ROBERTS *a drink.*) Here you are, Doug. (DOC *holds the drink up in a toast.*) To better days!

ROBERTS. Okay. And to a great American, Frank Thurlowe Pulver . . . Soldier . . . Statesman . . . Scientist . . .

DOC. Friend of the Working Girl . . . (*Suddenly there is a tremendous explosion.* DOC *and* ROBERTS *clutch at the desk.*) He wasn't kidding! That's fulminate of mercury!

CAPTAIN. (*Offstage.*) What was that? (ROBERTS *and* DOC *rush to porthole, listening.*)

JOHNSON. (*Offstage.*) I don't know, Captain. I'll find out. (*We hear the sounds of running feet.*)

ROBERTS. Doc, we've got to go down and get him.

DOC. This may be pretty bad, Doug. (*They turn to start for the door when suddenly a figure hurtles into the room and stops. For a moment it looks like a combination scarecrow and snowman but it is* PULVER—*his uniform tattered, his knees, arms and face blackened, he is covered with soapsuds and his eyes are shining with excitement.* ROBERTS *stares in amazement.*)

PULVER. Jeez, that stuff's terrific!

DOC. Are you all right?

PULVER. I'm great! Gee, you should've been there!

ROBERTS. You aren't burned—or anything?

PULVER. Hell, no. But the laundry's kinda beat up. All those washing machines are on the other side of the room now. And there's a new porthole on the starboard side where the electric iron went through. And I guess a steam-line must've busted or something—I was up to my ass in lather. And soapflakes flyin' around—it was absolutely beautiful! (*During these last lines,* DOC *has been making a brisk, professional examination.*) Come on down and see it, Doug. It's a Winter Wonderland!

CAPTAIN. (*Offstage.*) Johnson!

ROBERTS. Quiet!

JOHNSON. (*Offstage.*) Yes, sir.

CAPTAIN. (*Offstage.*) What was it?

JOHNSON. (*Offstage.*) The laundry, Captain. A steam-line must've blew up.

PULVER. (*Explaining.*) Steam-line shot right out of the bulkhead. (*He demonstrates.*) Whish!

CAPTAIN. (*Offstage.*) How much damage?

JOHNSON. (*Offstage.*) We can't tell yet, Captain. We can't get in there—the passageway is solid soapsuds.

PULVER. Solid soapsuds. (*He pantomimes walking blindly through soapsuds.*)

CAPTAIN. (*Offstage.*) Tell those men to be more careful.

57

ROBERTS. (*Excitedly.*) Frank, our celebration is just getting started. The night is young and our duty's clear.

PULVER. Yeah? What're we gonna do now, Doug?

ROBERTS. Get cleaned up and come with me.

PULVER. Where we goin' now, Doug?

ROBERTS. We're going down and get the rest of your stuff. You proved it'd work—you just hit the wrong target, that's all. We're going to make another firecracker, and put it where it really belongs.

PULVER. (*Who has slowly wilted during* ROBERTS' *speech.*) The rest of my stuff was—in the laundry, Doug. It all went up. There isn't any more. I'm sorry, Doug. I'm awful sorry.

ROBERTS. (*Sinks into chair.*) That's all right, Frank.

PULVER. Maybe I can scrounge some more tomorrow.

ROBERTS. Sure.

PULVER. You aren't sore at me, are you, Doug?

ROBERTS. What for?

PULVER. For spoilin' our celebration?

ROBERTS. Of course not.

PULVER. It was a good idea though, wasn't it, Doug?

ROBERTS. Frank, it was a great idea. I'm proud of you. It just didn't work, that's all. (*He starts for the door.*)

DOC. Where are you going, Doug?

ROBERTS. Out on deck.

PULVER. Wait'll I get cleaned up and I'll come with you.

ROBERTS. No, I'm going to turn in after that. (*To* PULVER.) It's okay, Frank. (*He exits.* PULVER *turns pleadingly to* DOC.)

PULVER. He was happy there for a minute though, wasn't he, Doc? Did you see him laughing? He was happy as hell. (*Pause.*) What's the matter with him anyhow, Doc? Did you find out?

DOC. No, he wouldn't tell me. But I know one thing he's feeling tonight and that's panic. Tonight he feels his war is dying before he can get to it. (DOC *goes to radio and turns up volume.*)

PULVER. I let him down. He wanted to celebrate and I let him down. (*He drops his head.* ANNOUNCER'S VOICE *on radio comes up as the lights*)

FADE OUT

(*During the darkness and under the first part of* SCENE 4 *we hear the voice of a British broadcaster:*)

BRITISH BROADCASTER. . . . . we hope that the King and the Queen will come out. The crowds are cheering—listen to them—and at any second now we hope to see Their Majesties. The color here is tremendous—everywhere rosettes, everywhere gay, red-white-and-blue hats. All the girls in their summer frocks on this lovely, mild, historic May evening. And although we celebrate with joyous heart the great victory, perhaps the greatest victory in the history of mankind, the underlying mood is a mood of thanksgiving. And now, I believe, they're coming. They haven't appeared but the crowd in the center are cheering madly. Handkerchiefs, flags, hands waving—HERE THEY COME! First, Her Majesty, the Queen, has come into view. Then the King in the uniform of an Admiral of the Fleet. The two Princesses standing on the balcony —listen to the crowd —— (*Sound of wild cheering. This broadcast continues throughout the blackout and the next scene. Several times the station is changed, from a broadcast of the celebration in San Francisco to the speaker in New York and the band playing " The Stars and Stripes Forever " in Times Square.*)

SCENE 4

The lights dim up on the main set. It is a few minutes later, and bright moonlight. The ship is under way— this is indicated by the apparent movement of the stars, slowly up and down. A group of men are sitting on the hatch cover in a late bull session. They are INSIGNA, MANNION, DOLAN and STEFANOWSKI. GERHART stands over them, he has obviously just returned from some mission for the group.

GERHART. A steam pipe busted in the laundry—they're cleaning it up now. It ain't worth going to see. (*The others make way for him and he sits down beside them. INSIGNA cocks his head toward the sound of the radio.*)
INSIGNA. What the hell's all that jabbering on the radio now?
MANNION. I don't know. Something about the King and Queen . . .
(*The men listen for a moment without curiosity, then, as the radio fades, they settle back in indolent positions.*)
INSIGNA. Well, anyhow, like I was telling you, this big sergeant in Elysium was scared to fight me! Tell 'em how big he was, Killer.

MANNION. Six foot seven or eight . . .

STEFANOWSKI. That sergeant's grown eight inches since we left Elysium. . . . Did you see me when I swiped that Shore Patrol band and went around arresting guys? That Shore Patrol officer said I was the best man he ever had.

MANNION. (*Smiles at* DOLAN *who is looking depressed.*) Come on, Dolan, don't let him get you down.

INSIGNA. Yeah, come on, Dolan. (ROBERTS *enters. He looks at the men, who have their backs turned, hesitates, then goes slowly over to them.*)

GERHART. (*Idly.*) What was them croquette things we had for chow tonight? (STEFANOWSKI *looks up and notices* ROBERTS. *Instantly he sits upright.*)

STEFANOWSKI. Flash Red! (*The men sit up. There is an embarrassed silence.*)

ROBERTS. Good evening. (*The men smile politely.* ROBERTS *is very embarrassed.*) Did you hear the news? The war's over in Europe.

MANNION. (*Smiling.*) Yes, sir. We heard.

STEFANOWSKI. (*Helping out the conversation.*) Sure. Maybe somebody'll get on the ball out here now . . . (DOLAN *rises, starts down hatchway.*)

ROBERTS. Dolan, I guess I kind of blew my top tonight. I'm sorry. I'm taking you off report.

DOLAN. Whatever you want, sir . . . (*He looks ostentatiously at his watch and yawns.*) Well, I guess I'll hit the old sack . . . (*He goes down hatchway.*)

MANNION. Yeah, me too . . .

INSIGNA. Yeah . . .

GERHART. It's late as hell.

STEFANOWSKI. I didn't realize how late it was . . . (*All the men get up, then go down the hatchway.* ROBERTS *stands looking after them. Now the radio is heard again.* ROBERTS *goes to hatchway and sits listening.*)

SPEAKER. . . . Our boys have won this victory today. But the rest is up to you. You and you alone must recognize our enemies: the forces of ambition, cruelty, arrogance and stupidity. You must recognize them, you must destroy them, you must tear them out as you would a malignant growth! And cast them from the surface of the earth! (*The end of the speech is followed by a band playing " The Stars and Stripes Forever."* ROBERTS' *face lights up and a new determination is in it. He repeats the words "malignant growth." The band music swells. He marches to the palm tree, salutes it, rubs his hands together and, as the music reaches a climax, he jerks the palm tree, earth and all, from the container and throws it over the side. Then, as the music continues, loud and climactic, he brushes his hands together, shrugs, and walks casually off L. singing the tune to himself. For a moment the stage is empty. Then the lights go up in the CAPTAIN'S cabin. The door to the CAPTAIN'S cabin opens and the CAPTAIN appears. He is in pajamas and bathrobe, and in one hand he carries his watering can. He discovers the empty container. He looks at it, then plunges into his cabin. After a moment, the General Alarm is heard. It is a terrible clanging noise designed to rouse the dead. When the alarm stops, the CAPTAIN'S voice is heard, almost hysterical, over the squawk box.)*

CAPTAIN. General Quarters! General Quarters! Every man to his battle station on the double! (*JOHNSON, in helmet and life jacket, scurries from hatchway into the CAPTAIN'S cabin. WILEY enters from R. passageway and climbs into the R. gun tub. Now men appear from all directions in various degrees of dress. The stage is filled with men frantically running everywhere, all wearing helmets and life preservers.*)

INSIGNA. (*Appearing from hatchway.*) What happened? (*He runs up the ladder and into the L. gun tub. PAYNE enters from L. and starts to climb up to L. gun tub.*) Get the hell out of here, Payne. This ain't your gun—your gun's over there!

DOLAN. (*Also trying to climb the ladder with PAYNE.*) Over there . . . over there . . . (*PAYNE crosses to R. gun tub.*)

REBER. (*Entering from hatchway.*) What the hell happened?

SCHLEMMER. Are we in an air raid?

PAYNE. Submarine . . . must be a submarine!

GERHART. Hey, Wiley, what happened?

DOWDY. (*Calling to someone on life raft.*) Hey, get away from that life raft. He didn't say abandon ship! (*During the confusion, STEFANOWSKI, bewildered, emerges from the hatchway and wanders over to R. gun tub.*)

STEFANOWSKI. Hey, Wiley, Payne—you sure you're supposed to be up there?

WILEY. Yeah.

STEFANOWSKI. (*Crossing to* L. *gun tub.*) Hey, Sam. Are you supposed to be up there?

INSIGNA. Yeah, we was here last year!

STEFANOWSKI. Hey, Dowdy. Where the hell's my battle station?

DOWDY. I don't know where your battle station is! Look around! (STEFANOWSKI *wanders aimlessly about.* WILEY, *in the gun tub* R., *is receiving reports of battle readiness from various parts of the ship:*)

WILEY. Twenty millimeters manned and ready. (*Pause.*) Engine room manned and ready. (*Pause.*) All battle stations manned and ready.

STEFANOWSKI. (*Sitting on corner of hatch.*) Yeah, all except mine . . .

JOHNSON'S VOICE. (*In* CAPTAIN'S *cabin.*) All battle stations manned and ready, Captain.

CAPTAIN'S VOICE. Give me that thing.

JOHNSON'S VOICE. ("*On mike*"—*that is, speaking directly into squawk-box microphone.* "*Off mike*" *means speaking unintentionally into this live microphone.*) Attention . . . Attention . . . The Captain wishes to . . .

CAPTAIN'S VOICE. (*Off mike.*) Give me that thing! (*On mike.*) All right, who did it? Who did it? You're going to stay here all night until someone confesses. You're going to stay at those battle stations until hell freezes over until I find out who did it. It's an insult to the honor of this ship! The symbol of our cargo record has been destroyed and I'm going to find out who did it if it takes all night! (*Off mike.*) Johnson, read me that muster list!

JOHNSON'S VOICE. (*Reading muster list off mike.*) Abernathy . . .

MANNION. Symbol of our cargo record? What the hell's that?	CAPTAIN'S VOICE. No, not Abernathy . . .
	JOHNSON'S VOICE. Baker . . .
(STEFANOWSKI *rises, sees empty container, kneels and ceremoniously bows to it.*)	CAPTAIN'S VOICE. No . . .
DOWDY. Stefanowski, find some battle station!	JOHNSON'S VOICE. Bartholomew . . . Becker . . . Billings . . .
(STEFANOWSKI *points to empty container.* DOWDY *sees it and*	Carney . . . Daniels . . . Dexter . . .

62

spreads the news to the men on L. SCHLEMMER *sees it and tells the other men. Now from all parts of the ship men enter and jubilantly look at the empty container. Bits of soil fly into the air as the men group around the empty can.)*

Ellison . . .

Everman . . .

Jenkins . . .

Kelly . . .

Kevin . . .

Martin . . .

Olsen . . .

O'Neill . . .

CAPTAIN'S VOICE. No, not O'Neill . . .

JOHNSON'S VOICE. Pulver . . .

CAPTAIN'S VOICE. No, not Pulver. He hasn't the guts . . .

JOHNSON'S VOICE. Roberts . . .

CAPTAIN'S VOICE. *(Roaring, off mike.)* Roberts! He's the one! Get him up here!

JOHNSON'S VOICE. *(On mike.)* Mister Roberts will report to the Captain's cabin on the double! *(The men rush back to their battle stations.)*

CAPTAIN'S VOICE. Get him up here, I tell you! Get him up here . . .

JOHNSON'S VOICE. *(On mike.)* Mister Roberts will report to the Captain's cabin on the . . .

CAPTAIN. *(Off mike.)* Give me that thing. *(On mike.)* Roberts, you get up here in a damn quick hurry. Get up here! Roberts, I'm giving you an order—get the lead out of your pants. *(ROBERTS appears from* L. *passageway and, walking slowly, enters the CAPTAIN'S cabin. The men move onstage and* LINDSTROM *gets to a position on the ladder where he can look through the porthole of the CAPTAIN'S cabin.)*

ROBERTS' VOICE. Did you want to see me, Captain?

CAPTAIN'S VOICE. You did it. You did it. Don't lie to me. Don't stand there and lie to me. Confess it!

ROBERTS' VOICE. Confess what, Captain? I don't know what you're talking about.

CAPTAIN'S VOICE. You know damn well what I'm talkin' about because you did it. You've doublecrossed me—you've gone back on your word!

ROBERTS' VOICE. No, I haven't, Captain.

CAPTAIN. Yes, you have. I kept my part of the bargain! I gave this

63

crew liberty—I gave this crew liberty, but you've gone back on your word. (DOWDY *takes off his helmet and looks at the men.*)

ROBERTS' VOICE. I don't see how you can say that, Captain. I haven't sent in any more letters. (DOLAN, *on gun tub ladder, catches* INSIGNA'S *eye.*)

CAPTAIN'S VOICE. I'm not talkin' about your sons-a-bitchin' letters. I'm talkin' about what you did tonight.

ROBERTS' VOICE. Tonight? I don't understand you, Captain. What do you think I did?

CAPTAIN. Quit saying that, dammit, quit saying that. You know damn well what you did. You stabbed me in the back. You stabbed me in the back . . . aaa . . . aa . . .

JOHNSON'S VOICE. Captain! Get over to the washbasin, Captain!

CAPTAIN'S VOICE. Aaaaaaa . . .

INSIGNA. What the hell happened?

DOLAN. Quiet!

JOHNSON. (*On mike.*) Will the Doctor please report to the Captain's cabin on the double? (DOC *appears from* L., *pushing his way through the crowd, followed by two* MEDICAL CORPSMEN *wearing Red Cross brassards and carrying first-aid kits and a stretcher.* DOC *walks slowly, he is idly attaching a brassard and smoking a cigarette. He wears his helmet sloppily.*)

DOC. Gangway . . . gangway . . .

DOWDY. Hey, Doc, tell us what's going on.

DOC. Okay. Okay. (*He enters the* CAPTAIN'S *cabin followed by the* CORPSMEN *who leave stretcher leaning against the bulkhead. The door closes. There is a tense pause. The men gather around the cabin again.* LINDSTROM *is at the porthole.*)

REBER. Hey, Lindstrom, where's the Old Man?

LINDSTROM. He's sittin' in the chair—leaning way forward.

PAYNE. What's the Doc doin'?

LINDSTROM. He's holdin' the waste basket.

REBER. What waste basket?

LINDSTROM. The one the Old Man's got his head in. And he needs it too. Oops! There he goes again. (*Pause.*) They're helpin' him over to the couch and they're takin' off his shoes. (*Pause.*) Look out, here they come. (*The men break quickly and rush back to their battle stations. The door opens and* ROBERTS, DOC *and the* CORPSMEN *come out.*)

DOC. (*To* CORPSMEN.) We won't need that stretcher. Sorry. (*Calls.* DOWDY *comes down to* DOC. *He avoids* ROBERTS' *eyes.*)

ROBERTS. Dowdy, pass the word to the crew to secure from General Quarters.

DOC. And tell the men not to make any noise while they go to their bunks. The Captain's resting quietly now, and I think that's desirable. (DOWDY *passes the word to the crew who slowly start to leave their battle stations. They are obviously stalling.* DOC, *to* ROBERTS.) Well, guess I'd better get back inside. I'll be down to see you after I get through. (*He enters cabin and stands there watching. The men move offstage, very slowly, saying "Good night, Mister Roberts," "Good night, sir." Suddenly* ROBERTS *notices that all the men are saying good night to him.*)

DOLAN. (*Quietly.*) Good night, Mister Roberts. (ROBERTS *does not hear him.*) Good night, Mister Roberts.

ROBERTS. Good night, Dolan. (DOLAN *smiles and exits down hatch.* ROBERTS *steps toward hatch, removes helmet, looks puzzled as the lights*)

FADE OUT

(*During the darkness, over the squawk box the following announcements are heard:*)

FIRST VOICE. Now hear this . . . Now hear this . . . C, E and S Divisions and all Pharmacist's Mates will air bedding today—positively!

SECOND VOICE. There is now available at the ship's store a small supply of peanut brittle. Ship's store will be open from 1300 to 1315.

THIRD VOICE. Now, Dolan, Yeoman Second Class, report to the radio shack immediately.

SCENE 5

The lights come up on the stateroom of ROBERTS *and* PULVER. PULVER *is lying in the lower bunk.* DOC *is sitting at the desk with a glass and a bottle of grain alcohol in front of him.* ROBERTS *is tying up a sea bag. A small suitcase stands beside it. His locker is open and empty.* WILEY *picks up the sea bag.*

WILEY. Okay, Mister Roberts. I'll take these down to the gangway. The boat from the island should be out here any minute for you. I'll let you know.

ROBERTS. Thanks, Wiley.

WILEY. (*Grinning.*) That's okay, Mister Roberts. Never thought you'd be taking this ride, did you? (*He exits with the bags.*)

ROBERTS. I'm going to be off this bucket before I even wake up.

DOC. They flying you all the way to the *Livingston?*

ROBERTS. I don't know. The radio dispatch just said I was transferred and travel by air if possible. I imagine it's all the way through. They're landing planes at Okinawa now and that's where my can is probably running around. (*Laughs a little.*) Listen to me, Doc—my can!

PULVER. (*Studying map by* ROBERTS' *bunk.*) Okinawa! Jeez, you be damn careful, Doug.

ROBERTS. Okay, Frank. This is too much to take, Doc. I even got a destroyer! The *Livingston!* That's one of the greatest cans out there.

PULVER. I know a guy on the *Livingston.* He don't think it's so hot.

DOLAN. (*Entering. He has a file folder under his arm.*) Here you are, Mister Roberts. I typed up three copies of the radio dispatch. I've got to keep a copy and here's two for you. You're now officially detached from this here bucket. Let me be the first.

ROBERTS. Thanks, Dolan. (*They shake hands.* ROBERTS *takes papers, and looks at them.*) Dolan, how about these orders? I haven't sent in a letter for a month!

DOLAN. (*Carefully.*) You know how the Navy works, Mister Roberts.

ROBERTS. Yeah, I know, but it doesn't seem . . .

DOLAN. Listen, Mister Roberts, I can tell you exactly what happened. Those guys at the Bureau need men for combat duty awful bad and they started looking through all the old letters and they just come across one of yours.

ROBERTS. Maybe—but still you'd think . . .

DOLAN. Listen, Mister Roberts. We can't stand here beating our gums! You better get cracking! You seen what it said there, "Proceed immediately." And the Old Man says if you ain't off of here in an hour, "I'll throw the son of a bitch off!"

ROBERTS. Is that all he said?

DOLAN. That's all he said.

ROBERTS. (*Grinning at* DOC.) After fighting this for two years you'd think he'd say more than that . . .

CAPTAIN'S VOICE. (*Offstage.*) Be careful of that one. Let it down easy.

DOC. What's that?

DOLAN. A new enlarged botanical garden. That's why he can't even be bothered about you today, Mister Roberts. Soon as we anchored this morning he sent Olsen over with a special detail— they dug up two palm trees . . . and you know what he's done— he's already set a twenty-four-hour watch on these new babies with orders to shoot to kill. (*To* PULVER.) That reminds me, Mister Pulver. The Captain wants to see you right away.

PULVER. Yeah? What about?

DOLAN. I don't know, sir. (*To* ROBERTS.) I'll be back to say good-bye, Mister Roberts. Come on, Mister Pulver. (*He exits.*)

PULVER. (*Following* DOLAN *out.*) I'll bet those bastards starched his pajamas again! (ROBERTS *smiles as he starts putting on his black tie.*)

DOC. You're a happy guy, aren't you?

ROBERTS. Yep. You're happy about it too, aren't you, Doc?

DOC. I think it's the only thing for you. (*Casually.*) What do you think of the crew now, Doug?

ROBERTS. We're all right now. I think they're nice guys—all of them.

DOC. Unh-hunh. And how do you think they feel about you?

ROBERTS. I think they like me all right . . . till the next guy comes along.

DOC. You don't think you're necessary to them?

ROBERTS. (*Sitting on bunk.*) Hell, no. No officer's necessary to the crew, Doc.

DOC. Are you going to leave this ship believing that?

ROBERTS. That's nothing against them, Doc. They're too busy looking out for themselves to care about anyone else.

DOC. Well, take a good, deep breath, Buster. (*He drinks some alcohol.*) What do you think got you your orders? Prayer and fasting? Sending in enough Wheatie box tops?

ROBERTS. My orders? Why, what Dolan said—one of my old letters turned up . . .

DOC. Bat crap! This crew got you transferred. They were so busy looking cut for themselves that they took a chance of landing in prison for five years—any one of them. Since you couldn't send in a letter for transfer, they sent one in for you. Since they knew the Captain wouldn't sign it approved, they didn't bother him—they signed it for him.

ROBERTS. What do you mean? They forged the Captain's name?

DOC. That's right.

ROBERTS. (*Rising.*) Doc! Who did? Which one of them?

DOC. That would be hard to say. You see, they had a mass meeting down in the compartment. They put guards at every door. They called it the Captain's-Name-Signing contest. And every man in this crew—a hundred and sixty-seven of them—signed the Captain's name on a blank sheet of paper. And then there were judges who compared these signatures with the Captain's and selected the one to go in. At the time there was some criticism of the decision on the grounds that the judges were drunk, but apparently, from the results, they chose well.

ROBERTS. How'd you find out about this, Doc?

DOC. Well, it was a great honor. I am the only officer aboard who does know. I was a contestant. I was also a judge. This double honor was accorded me because of my character, charm, good looks and because the medical department contributed four gallons of grain alcohol to the contest. (*Pauses.*) It was quite a thing to see, Doug. A hundred and sixty-seven guys with only one idea in their heads—to do something for Mister Roberts.

ROBERTS. (*After a moment.*) I wish you hadn't told me, Doc. It makes me look pretty silly after what I just said. But I didn't mean it, Doc. I was afraid to say what I really feel. I love those bastards, Doc. I think they're the greatest guys on this earth. All of a sudden I feel that there's something wrong—something terribly wrong—about leaving them. Doc, what can I say to them?

DOC. You won't say anything—you don't even know. When you're safely aboard your new ship I'm supposed to write and tell you about it. And at the bottom of the letter, I'm supposed to say, "Thanks for the liberty, Mister Roberts. Thanks for everything."

ROBERTS. Good Lord! (PULVER *enters, downcast.*)

PULVER. I'm the new Cargo Officer. And that's not all—I got to have dinner with him tonight. He *likes* me! (*There is a polite rap on the door.*)

DOC. Come in. (*Enter* PAYNE, REBER, GERHART, SCHLEMMER,

DOLAN and INSIGNA, *all carrying canteen cups except* INSIGNA *whose cup is in his belt. He carries a large, red fire extinguisher.*) What's this?

INSIGNA. Fire and rescue party. Heard you had a fire in here. (*All are looking at* ROBERTS.)

ROBERTS. No, but—since you're here—I ——

INSIGNA. Hell, we got a false alarm then. Happens all the time. (*Sets extinguisher on desk.*) In that case, we might as well drink this stuff. (*He fills their glasses from the fire extinguisher.*)

ROBERTS. What's in that, a new batch of jungle juice?

INSIGNA. Yeah, in the handy, new, portable container. Everybody loaded? (*All nod.*)

DOLAN. Go ahead, Sam.

INSIGNA. (*To* ROBERTS.) There's a story going around that you're leaving us. That right?

ROBERTS. (*Carefully.*) That's right, Sam. And I . . .

INSIGNA. Well, we didn't want you to get away without having a little drink with us and we thought we ought to give you a little sort of going-away present. The fellows made it down in the machine shop. It ain't much but we hope you like it. (REBER *prompts him.*) We all sincerely hope you like it. (*Calls offstage.*) All right, you bastards, you can come in now. (*Enter* LINDSTROM, MANNION, DOWDY *and* STEFANOWSKI. MANNION *is carrying a candy box. He walks over to* ROBERTS *shyly and hands him the box.*)

ROBERTS. What is it?

SCHLEMMER. Open it. (ROBERTS *opens the box. There is a deep silence.*)

PULVER. What is it, Doug? (ROBERTS *holds up the box. In it is a brass medal shaped like a palm tree attached to a piece of gaudy ribbon.*)

LINDSTROM. It's a palm tree, see.

DOLAN. It was Dowdy's idea.

DOWDY. Mannion here made it. He cut it out of sheet brass down in the machine shop.

INSIGNA. Mannion drilled the words on it too.

MANNION. Stefanowski thought up the words.

STEFANOWSKI. (*Shoving* LINDSTROM *forward.*) Lindstrom gets credit for the ribbon from a box of candy that his sister-in-law sent him. Read the words, Mister Roberts.

ROBERTS. (*With difficulty.*) "Order . . . order of . . ." (*He hands the medal to* DOC.)

DOC. (*Rises and reads solemnly.*) "Order of the palm. To Lieutenant (jg) Douglas Roberts for action against the enemy, above and beyond the call of duty ——" (*He passes the medal back to* ROBERTS.)

ROBERTS. (*After a moment—smiling.*) It's very nice but I'm afraid you've got the wrong guy. (*The men turn to* DOWDY, *grinning.*)

DOWDY. We know that, but we'd kinda like for you to have it anyway.

ROBERTS. All right, I'll keep it. (*The men beam. There is an awkward pause.*)

GERHART. Stefanowski thought up the words.

ROBERTS. They're fine words. (WILEY *enters.*)

WILEY. The boat's here, Mister Roberts. I put your gear in. They want to shove off right away.

ROBERTS. (*Rising.*) We haven't had our drink yet.

REBER. No, we ain't. (*All get to their feet.* ROBERTS *picks up his glass, looks at the crew, and everyone drinks.*)

ROBERTS. Good-bye, Doc.

DOC. Good-bye, Doug.

ROBERTS. And thanks, Doc.

DOC. Okay.

ROBERTS. Good-bye, Frank.

PULVER. Good-bye, Doug.

ROBERTS. Remember, I'm counting on you. (PULVER *nods.* ROBERTS *turns to the crew and looks at them for a moment. Then he takes the medal from the box, pins it on his shirt, shows it to them, then gives a little gestured salute and exits as the lights*)

FADE OUT

(*During the darkness we hear voices making announcements over the squawk box:*)

FIRST VOICE. Now hear this . . . now hear this . . . Sweepers, man your brooms. Clean sweep-down fore and aft!

SECOND VOICE. Now hear this! All men put on report today will fall in on the quarter-deck—and form three ranks!

THIRD VOICE. Now hear this! All divisions will draw their mail at 1700—in the mess hall.

The lights come up showing the main set at sunset. DOC is sitting on the hatch, reading a letter. MANNION, wearing sidearms, is pacing up and down in front of the CAPTAIN'S cabin. On each side of the door is a small palm tree in a five-gallon can—on one can is painted in large white letters, "Keep Away", on the other, "This Means You." After a moment, PULVER enters from the L. passageway, carrying a small packet of letters.

PULVER. Hello, Mannion. Got your mail yet?

MANNION. No, sir, I've got the palm tree watch.

PULVER. Oh. (*To* DOC.) What's your news, Doc?

DOC. My wife got some new wallpaper for the living room. (PULVER *sits on hatch cover.* DOWDY *enters wearing work gloves.*)

DOWDY. Mister Pulver, we'll be finished with the cargo in a few minutes.

PULVER. How'd it go?

DOWDY. Not bad. I've got to admit you were right about Number Three hold. It worked easier out of there. Mister Pulver, I just found out what the Captain decided—he ain't going to show a movie again tonight.

PULVER. Why not?

DOWDY. He's still punishing us because he caught Reber without a shirt on two days ago. You've got to go in and see him.

PULVER. I did. I asked him to show a movie yesterday.

DOWDY. Mister Pulver, what the hell good does that do us today? You've got to keep needlin' that guy—I'm tellin' you.

PULVER. Don't worry. I'll take care of it in my own way.

DOWDY. (*Going off, but speaking loud enough to be heard.*) Oh, hell, no movie again tonight. (*He exits.* PULVER *starts looking at his packet of mail.*)

PULVER. (*Looking at first letter.*) This is from my mother. All she ever says is stay away from Japan. (*He drops it on the hatch cover.*) This is from Alabama. (*Puts it in his pocket and pats it. Looks at third letter.*) Doc! This is from Doug!

DOC. Yeah? (PULVER *rips open the envelope.*) What does he say?

PULVER. (*Reading.*) "This will be short and sweet, as we're shoving off in about two minutes . . ." (*Pauses and remarks.*)

This is dated three weeks ago.

DOC. Does he say where he is?

PULVER. Yeah. He says: "My guess about the location of this ship was just exactly right." (*Looks up.*) That means he's around Okinawa all right! (*Reads on and chuckles.*) He's met Fornell. That's that friend of mine . . . a guy named Fornell I went to college with. Listen to this: "Fornell says that you and he used to load up your car with liquor in Omaha and then sell it at an indecent profit to the fraternity boys at Iowa City. How about that?" We did too. (*Smiles happily.*) "This part is for Doc." (DOC *gestures for him to read it.*) "I've been aboard this destroyer for two weeks now and we've already been through four air attacks. I'm in the war at last, Doc. I've caught up with that task force that passed me by. I'm glad to be here. I had to be here, I guess. But I'm thinking now of you, Doc, and you, Frank, and Dolan and Dowdy and Insigna and everyone else on that bucket —all the guys everywhere who sail from Tedium to Apathy and back again—with an occasional side trip to Monotony. This is a tough crew on here, and they have a wonderful battle record. But I've discovered, Doc, that the most terrible enemy of this war is the boredom that eventually becomes a faith and, therefore, a sort of suicide—and I know now that the ones who refuse to surrender to it must be very strong. Right now, I'm looking at something that's hanging over my desk: a preposterous hunk of brass attached to the most bilious piece of ribbon I've ever seen. I'd rather have it than the Congressional Medal of Honor. It tells me what I'll always be proudest of—that at a time in the world when courage counted most, I lived among a hundred and sixty-seven brave men. So, Doc, and especially you, Frank, don't let those guys down. Of course, I know that by this time they must be very happy because the Captain's overhead is filled with marbles and . . . (*He avoids* DOC's *eyes.*) Oh, hell, here comes the mail orderly. This has to go now. I'll finish it later. Meanwhile you bastards can write too, can't you? Doug."

DOC. Can I see that, Frank? (PULVER *hands him the letter, looks at the front of his next letter and says quietly:*)

PULVER. Well, I'll be damned, this is from Fornell.

DOC. (*Reading* ROBERTS' *letter to himself.*) ". . . I'd rather have it than the Congressional Medal of Honor." I'm glad he found that out. (*He looks at* PULVER, *sensing something wrong.*) What's the matter? (PULVER *does not answer.*) What's the matter, Frank? (PULVER *looks at him slowly as* DOWDY *enters.*)

DOWDY. All done, Mister Pulver. We've secured the hatch cover. No word on the movie, I suppose.

DOC. (*Louder, with terror.*) Frank, what is it?

PULVER. Mister Roberts is dead. (*Looks at letter.*) This is from Fornell . . . They took a Jap suicide plane. It killed everyone in a twin-forty battery and then it went on through and killed Doug and another officer in the wardroom. (*Pause.*) They were drinking coffee when it hit.

DOWDY. (*Quietly.*) Mister Pulver, can I please give that letter to the crew?

DOC. No. (*Holding out* ROBERTS' *letter.*) Give them this one. It's theirs. (DOWDY *removes gloves and takes the letter from* DOC *and goes off.*) Coffee . . . (PULVER *gets up restlessly.* DOC *stares straight ahead.* PULVER *straightens. He seems to grow. He walks casually over to* MANNION.)

PULVER. (*In a friendly voice.*) Go on down and get your mail. I'll stand by for you.

MANNION. (*Surprised.*) You will? Okay, thanks, Mister Pulver. (MANNION *disappears down hatch. As soon as he exits* PULVER *very calmly jerks the rooted palms, one by one, from their containers and throws them over the side.* DOC *looks up to see* PULVER *pull second tree.* DOC *ducks as tree goes past him. Then* PULVER *knocks loudly on the* CAPTAIN'S *door.*)

PULVER. Captain!

CAPTAIN. (*Offstage. His voice is very truculent.*) Yeah. Who is it?

PULVER. This is Ensign Pulver. I just threw your palm trees overboard. Now what's all this crap about no movie tonight? (*He throws the door open, banging it against the bulkhead, and is entering the* CAPTAIN'S *cabin as*)

THE CURTAIN FALLS

PROPERTIES

ACT I—SCENE 1
Set Props

D. R.: Double bitt

L. on rail: Life raft (painted on drop)

R. gun turret: 20 mm. gun with (canvas cover optional) 1 pair asbestos gloves

R. of Captain's door, on deck: Palm tree in 5 gal. square can, hinged to pedestal, painted green, with lettering, " Prop't of Captain, Keep Away; " pedestal 14" high for palm to stand on, hinged to deck; ventilator R. of palm; between portholes—communications set

Hand Props

U. R.: Pencil (Roberts); letter—rough copy on yellow paper (Roberts); work gloves (Roberts) (wardrobe)

U. C.: 1 gal. oil can with water—type used to fill autos (Captain)

U. L.: Plug chewing tobacco (Johnson), licorice or coke may be used; police whistle (Johnson); stethoscope (Doc)

Under Stage: Heavy Navy crockery coffee cup (Dowdy); 2 wire brushes (Dowdy); 3 rust scrapers (Dowdy); work gloves (Dowdy) (wardrobe)

On Bridge R.: 1 Navy telescope (Schlemmer); 4 Navy binoculars (Schlemmer); lens cleaner—several sheets (Schlemmer)

ACT I—SCENE 2
Set Props

D. R.: Navy locker, stencilled " Lt. (jg) D. A. Roberts." On top locker: Metal basket holding miscellaneous books, papers, etc. Inside locker—top shelf: Miscellaneous books, hats, etc. Inside locker—on hangers: Several uniforms (wardrobe); outside uniform, nearest audience, should be khaki hung with trousers and blouse and hat in such a way as to indicate, at a casual glance, that someone is standing there. Inside locker—on floor: Many dirty scivvy shirts and drawers (wardrobe). Inside of locker door: Pocketed cloth shoe container holding shoes, whisk broom and other accessories

Against R. wall—U. S. of locker: Double-tiered bunk with four drawers below lower bunk: Upper bunk—Pulver's: Mattress, pillow, bedspread covering pillow and sewed to mattress; plywood bottom to bunk; Navy blanket folded at foot of bunk. Under mattress: Small tin tobacco can containing 5 marbles; 1 cardboard center from roll toilet paper; 1 piece twine 14" long; 1 bottle Coca Cola; pocket book edition of " God's Little Acre." On wall, over bunk: Various pinups, etc. Accessories to upper bunk: Ashtray on collapsible extension arm; extra-long goose-neck lamp (electrics). Lower bunk—Roberts: Mattress, pillow, bedspread sewed to mattress

Navy blanket folded at foot of bunk; 2 square souvenir pillows against wall C. of bunk: 1 pillow lettered " Toujours L'Amour, Souvenir of San Diego —oo-la-la." Plain back. 1 pillow lettered " Compliments of Allis-Chalmers — Farm Equipment — We Plow Deep While Others Sleep." Plain back. On wall, behind lower bunk: Maps of European and Pacific war zones (April, 1945)

Against U. L. wall: Wash basin (not practical) with glass shelf above: 3 water glasses on shelf; medicine cabinet above basin containing: Bottles of iodine, Bromo Seltzer, Wildroot Wave Set, Eno's Fruit Salts, Kreml

74

Hair Tonic. D. S. of basin: Locker stencilled "Ens. F. T. Pulver" (not practical). On top locker: Electric fan (electrics). U. S. side of locker: Hook with bath towel; shaving mirror with extension. D. S. of locker: Desk: On top of desk: Pen set, miscellaneous papers in wooden file, basket with worn copy of magazine on top, glass ashtray, water glass, goose-neck lamp (electrics), radio (sound). Drawer of desk equipped with bottle opener in handle. In drawer: Reserve bottle opener, matches, stopper, Coca Cola cap. U. S.: Desk straight chair, green leather back and seat. Below desk another straight chair, similar. D. S.: On stage corner of desk: Plain metal basket with quart vinegar bottle almost full of water and stoppered. Over desk: Curtains around porthole, on rod

Hand Props

U. C.: Manila letter file folder containing Roberts' letter, in triplicate and with paper clips, typed on official stationery (Dolan)

ACT I—SCENE 3
Set Props

Same as Act I—Scene 1
Add: Cartons in cargo net; 24" megaphone on hatch (Roberts); clip-board with requisitions against D. L. corner hatch (Roberts)

Hand Props

D. R.: Requisition from L. C. T. (Dowdy); cargo net (men); heaving line (men). U. R. on bridge: Roberts' letter (Captain); Manila letter file folder (Dolan)

ACT I—SCENE 4—THE DECK
Set Props

Same as Act I—Scene 3

Hand Props

D. R.: 1 Navy spyglass (Insigna); 4 Navy binoculars (Mannion, Lindstrom, Wiley, Stefanowski) U. R.: Official Navy Sailing Directions for Pacific (Roberts); sailing orders (Roberts)

ACT I—SCENE 5
Set Props

D. R. corner: Straw broom
D. R. under porthole: Small bench. On bench: Battered magazines, shoe polish, brushes, shine cloths. Under bench: Piece of pipe
U. R. wall: "Varga Girl" pin-ups
U. R. corner: 3-tiered bunk, each tier with mattress, pillow and blanket. Under bottom bunk—net laundry bag —full ditty bag. Miscellaneous clothing strewn on bunks

Against L. wall: 3-tiered bunk, each tier with mattress, pillow and blanket; miscellaneous clothing strewn on bunks particularly to hide porthole in L. wall; under bottom bunk—full ditty bag; "Varga Girl" pin-ups on wall
U. C. corner: Squawk box on wall (sound)
D. C.: Bench with battered copy "True Detective" on seat (Dowdy)

75

Small hand-drawn map (Insignia)

Act I—Scene 6
Set Props

D. R.: Swivel armchair—leather

Against R. wall: Desk: On desk top: wooden file basket with papers, single letter (Roberts), pen set, lamp (electrics)

At wall end of desk: Stand holding: Switch panel for squawk box system with practical switch and pilot light (electrics) and practical microphone on small stand with extension cord (sound); switch panel for phone system with hand set—not practical

In R. wall above desk: Practical wall safe—Commander's cap inside

On R. wall above safe: Wall clock

U. C.—corner of L. wall: Locker—not practical

Against L. wall: Built-in settee, leather; rolls of charts lean against D. stage end of settee

Around portholes in L. wall: Curtains on rods

On L. wall: Small rack containing folded charts, etc., between portholes; small ship's model on shelf above D. S. end of settee

C. facing desk: Straight chair, leather

Act II—Scene 1
Set Props

Same Act I—Scene 3

Add: Desk U. R.: Log book; yellow slips on spindle; pencils

U. L. C.: Table (Doc's): Bandages, cotton dispenser, bottles, scissors, swabs, band-aids, adhesive tape, gauze, and box containing pro kits

On hatch: Yellow slips (Roberts)

Side Props

D. R.: Yellow slips (S. P.); goat with collar, name plate, and chain leash (Dolan); hand siren

Act II—Scene 2—The Deck
Set Props

Same as end of Act II—Scene 1

Hand Props

D. R.: Pen (Dolan); Manila file folder with: Directive; Roberts' letter

Act II—Scene 3
Set Props

Under Pulver's mattress: Firecracker

On desk: Bottle alcohol (same as vinegar bottle Act I—Scene 2); large can orange juice; 3 water glasses; old magazine

Off stage R.: Explosion effect barrel

Strike Off

Pulver's souvenir pillows

Off stage L.: (Soap suds equipment and electric mixer); 2 large rubber sheets —on floor; 2 large pans of soap suds; 1 pail of hot water—to soak Pulver's tattered uniform; 1 large wire mixer; 2 bath towels (3 dozen supply). Note: The following material was found most satisfactory for its adhering and lasting qualities: Nacconal L A L which may be obtained from National Aniline Division, Allied Chemical & Dye Corp., New York 6, N. Y.

Act II—Scene 4—The Deck

Set Props

(Same as other deck scenes.) (Note: duplicate palm tree—removable)

Side Props

D. R. off stage: Stretcher—Navy regulation

U. R. off stage: 1 pair binoculars

In R. stage gun turret: Ear phones

U. C. off stage: Watering can (Captain)

Act II—Scene 5—Roberts' Cabin

Set Props

Same as other Roberts' scenes

Add: On desk: Bottle of alcohol—same as before; 3 water glasses

D. R. on floor: Roberts' sea-bag (Wiley); Roberts' Val-Pak (Wiley)

D. stage top drawer of bunks: Black necktie (Roberts)

Strike

Wastebasket

Side Props

U. C.: Official orders in file folder (Dolan); 10 canteen cups (men); fire extinguisher containing orange juice (Insignia); cardboard candy box containing palm medal (Mannion)

Act II—Scene 6—The Deck

Set Props

Same as other deck scenes

Add: 2 palm trees in 5 gal. cans—one each side of door U. C. St. R. can lettered " Keep Away." St. L. can lettered " This Means You."

D. R. corner of hatch: Letter (Doc) (sample wall paper enclosed)

Side Props

U. L. off stage: Packet of letters tied with string (Pulver) (from top of packet letters are arranged as follows): 1—letter from mother, 2—Doug letter—practical, 3—Fornell letter—practical, 4—miscellaneous letter, 5—miscellaneous letter, 6—miscellaneous letter; leather gloves (Dowdy)

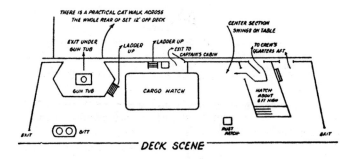

THERE IS A PRACTICAL CAT WALK ACROSS
THE WHOLE REAR OF SET 12' OFF DECK

CENTER SECTION
SWINGS ON TABLE

EXIT UNDER
GUN TUB

LADDER
UP

LADDER UP

EXIT TO
CAPTAIN'S CABIN

TO CREW'S
QUARTERS AFT

GUN TUB

CARGO HATCH

HATCH
ABOUT
6 FT HIGH

EXIT

BITT

RUST
PATCH

EXIT

DECK SCENE

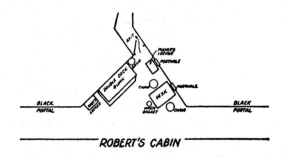

EXIT

PLAYER'S
LOCKER

PORTHOLE

DOUBLE DECK
BUNK

CHAIR

PORTHOLE

DESK

WASTE
BASKET

CHAIR

BLACK
PORTAL

BLACK
PORTAL

ROBERT'S CABIN

SCENE DESIGNS
"MISTER ROBERTS"

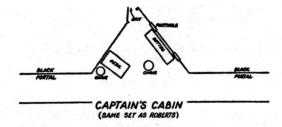

CAPTAIN'S CABIN
(SAME SET AS ROBERTS)

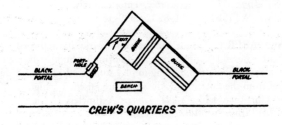

CREW'S QUARTERS

SCENE DESIGNS
"MISTER ROBERTS"

NEW PLAYS

★ **AUGUST: OSAGE COUNTY by Tracy Letts.** WINNER OF THE 2008 PULITZER PRIZE AND TONY AWARD. When the large Weston family reunites after Dad disappears, their Oklahoma homestead explodes in a maelstrom of repressed truths and unsettling secrets. "Fiercely funny and bitingly sad." *–NY Times.* "Ferociously entertaining." *–Variety.* "A hugely ambitious, highly combustible saga." *–NY Daily News.* [6M, 7W] ISBN: 978-0-8222-2300-9

★ **RUINED by Lynn Nottage.** WINNER OF THE 2009 PULITZER PRIZE. Set in a small mining town in Democratic Republic of Congo, RUINED is a haunting, probing work about the resilience of the human spirit during times of war. "A full-immersion drama of shocking complexity and moral ambiguity." *–Variety.* "Sincere, passionate, courageous." *–Chicago Tribune.* [8M, 4W] ISBN: 978-0-8222-2390-0

★ **GOD OF CARNAGE by Yasmina Reza, translated by Christopher Hampton.** WINNER OF THE 2009 TONY AWARD. A playground altercation between boys brings together their Brooklyn parents, leaving the couples in tatters as the rum flows and tensions explode. "Satisfyingly primitive entertainment." *–NY Times.* "Elegant, acerbic, entertainingly fueled on pure bile." *–Variety.* [2M, 2W] ISBN: 978-0-8222-2399-3

★ **THE SEAFARER by Conor McPherson.** Sharky has returned to Dublin to look after his irascible, aging brother. Old drinking buddies Ivan and Nicky are holed up at the house too, hoping to play some cards. But with the arrival of a stranger from the distant past, the stakes are raised ever higher. "Dark and enthralling Christmas fable." *–NY Times.* "A timeless classic." *–Hollywood Reporter.* [5M] ISBN: 978-0-8222-2284-2

★ **THE NEW CENTURY by Paul Rudnick.** When the playwright is Paul Rudnick, expectations are geared for a play both hilarious and smart, and this provocative and outrageous comedy is no exception. "The one-liners fly like rockets." *–NY Times.* "The funniest playwright around." *–Journal News.* [2M, 3W] ISBN: 978-0-8222-2315-3

★ **SHIPWRECKED! AN ENTERTAINMENT—THE AMAZING ADVENTURES OF LOUIS DE ROUGEMONT (AS TOLD BY HIMSELF) by Donald Margulies.** The amazing story of bravery, survival and celebrity that left nineteenth-century England spellbound. Dare to be whisked away. "A deft, literate narrative." *–LA Times.* "Springs to life like a theatrical pop-up book." *–NY Times.* [2M, 1W] ISBN: 978-0-8222-2341-2

DRAMATISTS PLAY SERVICE, INC.
440 Park Avenue South, New York, NY 10016 212-683-8960 Fax 212-213-1539
postmaster@dramatists.com www.dramatists.com